The Autobiography
of an American Novelist

18
33
45
72

Thomas Wolfe in 1935, at the time he wrote
The Story of a Novel. From a copy in
the North Carolina Collection of
the University of North
Carolina Library,
Chapel Hill.

THE
AUTOBIOGRAPHY
OF AN
AMERICAN
NOVELIST

Thomas Wolfe

Edited by Leslie Field

HARVARD UNIVERSITY PRESS
Cambridge, Massachusetts
London, England
1983

Library of Congress Cataloging in Publication Data

Wolfe, Thomas, 1900–1938.
 The autobiography of an American novelist.

 Consists of two autobiographical essays: The story of a novel and Writing and living.
  1. Wolfe, Thomas, 1900–1938.   2. Novelists, American —20th century—Biography.   3. Fiction—Authorship.
I. Field, Leslie A.   II. Wolfe, Thomas, 1900–1938. Writing and living. 1983.   III. Title.
PS3545.O336Z474   1983   813'.52 [B]   82–21285
ISBN 0–674–05316–8
ISBN 0–674–05317–6 (pbk.)

Contents

Preface
vii

The Story of a Novel
1

Writing and Living
91

Preface

IN THESE AUTOBIOGRAPHICAL ESSAYS, BROUGHT TOGETHER IN
their original form for the first time, Thomas Wolfe's subject
is creativity. Of his generation of writers—including
Faulkner, Fitzgerald, Hemingway—he alone attempted to explain the creative process of the artist. Here, he shares with his
audience that process.

In so doing, Wolfe was like his great nineteenth-century
predecessors Mark Twain and Henry James, who also tried to
convey how the novelist transmutes experience and mind in
creating fiction. His portrayal of the role of the writer both
resembled and often went beyond that of his contemporaries.
Like Faulkner, he felt compelled to depict his view of the
South: black versus white, the Civil War, the pull of the land,
Yoknapatawpha. Like Fitzgerald, he wrote of the Lost Generation, the Jazz Age, wealth, the elusiveness of the American
dream. He admired Hemingway's creation of the hero, the
code of manliness, grace under pressure.

But perhaps Wolfe is really closer to Walt Whitman. Like
Whitman, Wolfe was a romantic who moved from a preoccupation with himself to an interest in his family, his friends, his
town, his America, and finally the larger, external world.
Wolfe explored time, faith, loneliness, and death; isolation,
alienation, change, experience; the city versus the country; the
North versus the South; the structure of society; the limits of
folklore, language, rhetoric, symbolism, humor, satire.

These concerns run through all of Wolfe's fiction, from
his first and most famous novel, *Look Homeward, Angel* (1929),

and his enormously long second book, *Of Time and the River* (1935), to his posthumously published books *The Web and the Rock* (1939) and *You Can't Go Home Again* (1940). They also resonate in his collection of short stories *From Death to Morning* (1935) and in the posthumous *The Hills Beyond* (1941).

While these major interests defined Wolfe's life, his belief that writing was a serious craft shaped his art. Through it he planned to encompass and convey his vision of the world. And so in *The Story of a Novel* and *Writing and Living* Wolfe tried to explain how a writer thinks and then goes about writing. "My conviction is," he said, "that all serious work must be at the bottom autobiographical, and that a man must use the material and experience of his own life if he is to create anything that has substantial value." Late in life Wolfe continued to wrestle with charges that he made excessive use of autobiography in his fiction. In a letter to Elizabeth Nowell, his literary agent, he once summed up his position. As usual he was thinking of facts—in this instance, an address he delivered to students—and his fictional rendering of those facts. He wrote, "That is what I am doing now, transforming . . . material . . . into the terms of poetic and imaginative fact—into the truth of fiction—because it seems to me that is really my essential job." In a word, Wolfe was translating *fact* into what he considered *truth*.

IN THE SUMMER OF 1935 Thomas Wolfe was invited to lecture at the University of Colorado's Writer's Conference. In preparation for his talk he formulated working titles such as "Some Problems of a Writer" and "The Artist in America," but he also had on hand his original preface to *Of Time and the River*. He drew upon this unpublished material as well as other ideas for the lecture, which ultimately became a typescript of seventy-four pages.

Wolfe received $250 in addition to payment of all expenses for a trip to the West. At his first stop, the State Teacher's College in Greeley, Colorado, he delivered one version of his talk. At Boulder, the conference was already in progress when Wolfe arrived, with Robert Frost, Robert Penn Warren, Martha Foley, and other literary people and scholars participating. When Wolfe's turn came, he spoke for an hour and forty minutes to an enthusiastic audience.

Before leaving for Colorado, Wolfe gave the manuscript, now called *The Story of a Novel*, to Elizabeth Nowell. After cutting it from fifteen thousand to seven thousand words, she sold it to the *Atlantic Monthly*. When Wolfe returned to New York, however, he informed her she had submitted only half of the manuscript; he had another fifteen thousand words. Although Nowell considerably reduced this portion too, the *Atlantic* would not publish the full essay because it was too long. Finally, the *Saturday Review of Literature* published the whole manuscript as edited by Nowell in its 1935 issues of December 14, 21, and 28. When Scribner's agreed to bring out *The Story of a Novel* as a small book, Wolfe expanded the *Saturday Review* essays and replaced many, but not all, of the portions that Nowell had originally cut. The book was published in this incomplete form in April 1936 by Scribner's.

In the spring of 1938 Wolfe was invited to speak at the annual Literary Awards Banquet at Purdue University on May 19 in West Lafayette, Indiana. He accepted eagerly and was pleased with the honorarium of $300. He intended to make Purdue the first stop on his second westward journey, this time to visit the national parks and to write about them.

Whereas at Boulder Wolfe had been one among several lecturers, at Purdue he was the sole speaker. His predecessors in that role were illustrious: Carl Sandburg, Sherwood Anderson, and Theodore Dreiser.

This was Wolfe's last public appearance, and his talk, entitled "Writing and Living," was his last formal public statement. In letters, Wolfe revealed that he considered his speech an important declaration about his writing. It was designed to fulfill a dual purpose: whereas Wolfe clearly started by addressing an audience of students at Purdue, he changed his point of view midway and began obviously composing the epilogue for the novel that became *You Can't Go Home Again*. Wolfe's Purdue speech was as successful as his Boulder talk had been.

Taken together in their original versions, published here for the first time, *The Story of a Novel* and *Writing and Living* constitute Thomas Wolfe's major statements about his life and his art. They are similar in many respects. In both he wanted to define the role of the writer in America. In both he emphasized that a writer is a *worker* and must be regarded as such. In both he insisted that there were no easy formulas for writing. In both he also wanted to convey the importance of autobiography to his fiction and how he legitimately used the facts of his life.

But there are also differences. In *The Story of a Novel* he was more concerned with discussing the romantic themes he saw as important to his early work: the themes of permanence and change, and man's search for a spiritual father. And he wanted to share with his audience and readers the close editor-author relationship that went into creating *Of Time and the River*. In *Writing and Living* Wolfe revealed his growth, his movement away from the romantic egocentrism of his youthful period to a new awareness of life outside himself, and his new social consciousness. Now, Wolfe believed that his earlier themes were no longer crucial. He realized that as a beginning writer he had been too narcissistic, too much the sensitive artist divorced from his environment. Late in his short life he saw the need for moving outside himself, for looking at the political, social, and economic world, and for trying to understand it, assimilate it, and somehow bring it into his writing. This, in fact, he attempted in his last novel, *You Can't Go Home Again.*

Taken together these two essays capture the essence of a writer's life and how it is molded into fiction. They form *The Autobiography of an American Novelist*, a significant statement by an important American writer, his candid commentary on his craft.

Leslie Field
West Lafayette, Indiana

A Note on the Manuscripts and Editorial Method

The history of composition and editing of *The Story of a Novel* and *Writing and Living* is not complicated. The former originated in the Boulder talk, subsequently was cut considerably, then accepted in one form by the *Saturday Review*, and ultimately re-edited by Wolfe before it appeared in the book published by Scribner's in 1936. Wolfe's original uncut manuscript is in the William B. Wisdom Collection of the Houghton Library at Harvard University; what appears here are Wolfe's original seventy-four pages of typed text, and some subsequent additions, never before published in their entirety.

Writing and Living was not published until July 1964. It was edited by William Braswell and Leslie Field from an unfinished typescript of sixty-three pages, punctuated and corrected by Wolfe's typist. It is a typescript which Wolfe revised slightly, but one which he would have polished even more. Braswell and Field found that part of this typescript, housed at the University of North Carolina Library, was missing (manuscript pages 18–24). It was located in the manuscript of *You Can't Go Home Again* at Harvard. Some pages are torn, and thus there are hiatuses in the text. There are also several additions and deletions in Wolfe's hand, and other alterations penciled in by Wolfe's typist and the editor of his posthumous works, Edward C. Aswell, of Harper's. The text here presented is that published in 1964—with the hiatuses filled in—as *Thomas Wolfe's Purdue Speech: "Writing and Living"* (Purdue University Studies).

In preparing *The Autobiography of an American Novelist* for publication, spelling and punctuation have been modernized and made consistent, occasional redundancies have been removed, and a few long paragraphs have been subdivided.

L.F.

The Autobiography
of an American Novelist

The Story of a Novel

A page of manuscript for *The Story of a Novel*, in Wolfe's handwriting. Reprinted by permission of the Houghton Library, Harvard University.

I T HAS BEEN SUGGESTED TO me that I talk to you upon the subject "The Making of a Book," and I am delighted to attempt a talk upon this subject because it has a pertinence and a direct relation to my own experience which topics of a critical or academic sort do not have.

A very great editor, who is also a very good friend of mine, told me about six months ago that he was sorry he had not kept a diary—a kind of daily journal—about the work that both of us were doing, the transaction that occurred, the whole stroke and catch, the flow, the stop, the cut, the molding, the whole ten thousand meetings, gratings, changings, surrenders, triumphs, and agreeings that went into the making of the book. This man, this editor that I have spoken of, remarked to me when all was over that some of it was fantastic and incredible, and he was also generous and kind enough to remark that the whole experience was the most interesting that he had known during the almost thirty years he had been a member of the publishing business.

I propose to tell you about this experience. I believe that if anything I can say to you may have value or interest, it will be somehow related to the facts of this experience. I am not really a professional writer. I do not feel that I can talk to you about the trends in the modern novel or attempt to tell you what the modern novelist is doing or attempt an analysis of what he has done the last five or ten years or what he will do in the five or ten which are to come. I cannot tell you how to write books; I cannot attempt to give you rules and suggestions whereby you will be enabled to get your books published by publishers or your stories accepted by popular and high-paying magazines. Yet all these things have happened to me. I have had my books accepted by a publisher and recently some of my stories were accepted by popular and high-priced magazines, but I do not know any rules for telling you how this can be accomplished. I am not a professional writer; I am not even a skilled writer; I am just a writer who is on the way to learning his profession and to discovering the line, the structure, and the articulation of the language which I must discover if I do the work I want to do. It is for just this reason, because I blunder, because my life and every energy of my life and talent are still involved in this process of discovery, this need for an assured and final articulation, this constant search for the discovery of a language which every man must find out for himself that I am talking to you as I talk to you tonight.

I am going to tell you, so far as I can in the special time that is given to me and as truthfully as I can remember, the way in which I wrote a book. It will be intensely personal. It came out of the substance of my life. It was the greatest and most intense part of my life for several years. It cost me the most intense effort, sweat, doubt, and suffering that I ever knew. There is nothing very literary about my story. It is a story of sweat and pain and despair and partial achievement. I did not achieve what I wanted to achieve; I failed in a way, which only I know about, and I came through, too. I don't know how to write a story yet. I don't know how to write a novel yet. Of all the people here in this audience, I am the last, the worst, the least prepared to tell anyone how to write a story in such a way that it will sell to anything, no matter what. But I have learned something about myself and about the work of writing, and if I can, I am going to try to tell you what it is.

It takes me a long time to tell things. A good many friendly critics have told me this, and I know that it is true. Sometimes it take me a good long time to get started. All of these thing are true; a great many penetrating and sympathetic people have told me so; I know it; I realize it, and I am going to try to learn and do better, but right now I will have to tell you about this thing in my own way, and to tell you in that way, I will have to go back, not only to what was perhaps the beginning of the book, but before the beginning of the book.

I don't know when I began to write or when it occurred to me first that I would be a writer. I suppose that like a great many other children in this country of my generation, I may have thought that it would be a fine thing to be a writer because a writer was a man like Lord Byron or Lord Tennyson or Longfellow or Percy Bysshe Shelley. A writer was a man who was far away like these people I have mentioned, and since I was, myself, an American and an American not of the wealthy or university or capitalized sort of people, it seemed to me that a writer was a man from a kind of remote and unknowable people that I could never approach.

I think this has happened to us all—or almost all of us here in America. We're still more perturbed and haunted by the strangeness of the writing profession than any other people I have seen or known on the earth. It is for this reason, I think, that one finds among a great number of our people, I mean the laboring, farming sort of people from which I came, a kind of great wonder and doubt and romantic feeling about writers so that it is hard for them to understand that a writer may be one of them and not a man far away like Lord Byron and Tennyson and Percy Bysshe Shelley. Then there is another kind of American who has come from the more educated, university-going kind of people, and these people also become fascinated with the glamor and the remoteness and difficulty of writing but in a different way. They get more involved or fancy than the most involved and fancy European people of this sort. They become more "Flauberty" than Flaubert. They establish little magazines that not only split a hair with the best of them, but they split more hairs than Europeans think of splitting. The Europeans say: "Oh God where did these people, these aesthetic Americans come from?" Well, we have known it all. I think all of us who have tried to write in this country may have fallen in between these two groups of well meaning and misguided people, and if we become writers, finally, it is in spite of each of them.

I don't know how I became a writer, but I think it was because of a certain force in me that had to write and that finally, like some kind of energy or torrent or pent power, burst through and found a channel. My people, as I have told you, were of the working class of people. My father, a stone-cutter, was a man with a great respect and veneration for literature. He had a tremendous memory, and he loved poetry, and the poetry that he loved best was naturally poetry of the sound and rhetorical kind that such a man would like. Nevertheless it was good poetry, Hamlet's soliloquy, *Macbeth*, Mark Antony's funeral oration, Grey's "Elegy," and all the rest of it. I heard it all as a child; I memorized and learned it all.

He sent me to college to the state university. The desire to write, to put words down on paper, which had been strong during all my days in high school, grew stronger still. I was editor of the college paper, the college magazine, etc., and in my last year or two at college I was a member of a course in playwriting which had just been established there. I wrote several little one-act plays, still thinking I would become a lawyer or a newspaper man, never daring, dreaming, hoping, to believe I could seriously become a writer. Then I went to Harvard, wrote some more plays there, which were put on in the Harvard playwriting group of that time, became obsessed then with the idea that I must, had to be, a playwright, left Harvard, had my plays rejected, and finally in the autumn of 1926, how, why, or in what manner I have never exactly been able to determine, I began to write my first book in London. I was living all alone at that time. I had two rooms — a bedroom and a sitting room — in a little square in Chelsea in which all the houses had that familiar, smoked brick, and cream-yellow-plaster look of London houses. They looked exactly alike.

As I say, I was living alone at the time and in a foreign country. I did not know why I was there or what the purpose or direction of my life should be, and that was the way I began to write my book. I think that is one of the hardest times a writer goes through. There is no standard, no outward judgment, no appraisal by which he can measure what he has done. By day I would write for hours in big ledgers which I had bought for the purpose; then at night, when I would try to sleep, I would lie in bed and fold my hands behind my head and think of what I had done that day and hear the solid, leather footbeat of the London bobby as he came by my window, and that utterly quiet London square, and wait until he had gone and remember that I was born in North Carolina and wonder why the hell I was now in London lying in the darkened bed, my hands beneath my head, and thinking about words I had that day put down on paper. I would get a great, hollow, empty, utterly futile feeling inside me, and then I would get up and go out into my sitting room and switch on the light and open up my ledgers and read the words I had written there that day, and then I would wonder: why am I here now? why have I come?

By day there would be the great, dull roar of London, the gold, yellow foggy light you have there in October. The man-swarmed and old, web-like, smoky, billion-footed London! And I loved the place, and I loathed it and abhorred it. I knew no one there, and I had been a child in North Carolina long ago, and I was living there in two rooms in the huge octopal and illimitable web of that overwhelming city. I did not know why I had come, why I was there.

I lived there several months and worked there every day with these feelings that I have described, and came back to America in the winter and worked here and for the next two years taught and worked. I would teach all day and write all night, although for one of these years I did nothing but write, and finally about two and a half years after I had begun the book in London, I finished it in New York.

I should like to tell you about this, too. I was very young at the time, and I had that kind of wild, exultant vigor which a man has at that period of his life. The book took hold of me and possessed me. In a way, I think it shaped itself. Like every young man, I was strongly under the influence of writers I admired. One of the chief writers at that time was Mr. James Joyce with his book *Ulysses*. I was a great deal under his spell. The book that I was writing was much influenced, I believe, by his own book, and yet the powerful energy and fire of my own youth played over and, I think, possessed it all. Like Mr. Joyce, I wrote about things that I had known, the immediate life and experience that had been familiar to me in my childhood. Unlike Mr. Joyce, I had no literary experience. I had never had anything published before. I had never really, even with the plays at North Carolina and Harvard, consigned my life and talent utterly to the work of writing. My feeling toward writers, publishers, books, that whole mysterious and fabulous world of printing, was almost as far away as when I was a child in North Carolina. I had seen pictures in my father's books of poetry of Lord Byron and Lord Tennyson. And yet my book, the world, the characters with which I had peopled it, the color and weather of the universe which I had created, had possessed me, and so I wrote and wrote with that bright and burning flame with which a young man writes who never has been published, and who yet is sure all will be so good all must be well. This is a curious thing and hard to tell about, yet quick and easy to understand in every writer's mind. I wanted fame, as every youth who ever wrote must want it, and yet fame was a bright and most uncertain thing.

I wrote always because I knew my writing must be read, and yet I never knew its public. I never knew what people it would reach; I never knew the end or goal or destination of my effort, but this great flame of energy and wild creation kept burning for two years or more, and I knew that *they* must take it, read it, like it, hold me in esteem — not knowing all the time who "they" might be. I am certain it must have been this way with every writer who ever lived, who ever began to write, who ever wrote his first book in utter obscurity, but who was sustained all the time by the flame of this wild and burning and indestructible hope, and the reason I am telling it to you is that you, if you have never written and published your first book before, must know it, too, because it is the first, the essential, and the incomparable experience that goes with the making of a writer. I won't tell you much more about this first book. What I have tried to tell you is that while I was writing it, although I knew no publisher, could not visualize or see a public, had no concrete or material experience with any of the methods of production and fulfillment, I wrote the book because I was sure it had a public, because I was sure it would have its final and complete fulfillment, without which a book is nothing. And yet all this was a kind of dream. The whole writing and publishing profession still seemed as far and remote as when I was a child and had seen the pictures of Byron and Tennyson in my father's books of poetry. It was only under the drunken illusion of creation that I saw the book as a powerful and accomplished fact, printed, published, and esteemed by the people, the rare, the fine, the wonderful people whose honor and respect I hoped it might win throughout the world.

The book was finished in my twenty-eighth year. I knew no publishers and no writers. A friend of mine took the huge manuscript — it was about 350,000 words long — and sent it to a publisher whom she knew. In a few days, a week or two, I received an answer from this man saying that the book could not be published. He said that his house had published five books like it the year before, that all of them had failed, and that, further, the book in its present form was so amateurish, autobiographical, and unskillful that a publisher could not risk a chance on it. I was, myself, so depressed and weary by this time, the first blow, the illusion of creation which had sustained me for two and a half years had so far worn off, that I believed what the man said. It seemed to fulfill and put the stamp of actual finality upon my own opinion. At that time I was a teacher in one of New York's great universities, and when the year came to a close, I went abroad. It was only after I had been abroad almost six months that news came to me from another publisher in America that he had read my manuscript and would like to talk to me about it as soon as I came home.

I came home on New Year's Day that year. The next day I called up the publisher who had written me. He asked me if I would come to his office and talk to him. I went at once, and before I had left his office that morning, I had signed a contract and had a check for five hundred dollars in my hand.

I don't suppose that experience is included in the usual course for writers, but it taught me a great deal. It was the first time, so far as I can remember, that anyone had concretely suggested to me that anything I had written was worth as much as fifteen cents, and I know that I left the publisher's office that day and entered into the great swarm of men and women who passed constantly along Fifth Avenue at 48th Street and that presently I found myself at 110th Street, and from that day to this I have never known how I got there.

For the next six or eight months I taught at the city university I mentioned and worked upon the manuscript of my book with this great editor. The book appeared in the month of October, 1929. The whole experience still had elements of that dream-like terror and unreality that writing had had for me when I had first begun it seriously and had lain in my room in London with my hands below my head and thought, why am I here now? The awful, utter nakedness of print, that thing which is for all of us so close akin, so namelessy akin to shame and guilt, came closer day by day. That I had wanted this exposure, I could not believe. I had so shamelessly exposed myself and yet it held me like a serpent's eye, and I could do no other. I turned to him at last, this editor who had worked with me and found me, and I asked him if he could foretell the end and verdict of my labor. He said that he would rather tell me nothing, that he could not prophesy or know what profit I would have. He said, "all that I know is that they cannot let it go, they cannot ignore it. The book will find its way."

And that fairly describes what happened. I have read in recent months, in certain magazines and reviews, that this first book was received with what is called a "storm of critical applause," but this really did not happen. The book was a first book by an unknown writer. It got some wonderful reviews in some places; it got some very unfavorable reviews in others, but the book made friends, and it unquestionably did have a good reception for a first book, and what was best of all, as time went on, it continued to make friends among people who read books. It showed an extraordinary vitality and continued to sell over a period of four or five years in the publisher's edition, and later in the cheaper edition, The Modern Library, it renewed its life and began to sell again. The upshot of it was that after the publication of this book in the autumn of 1929, I found myself with a position as a writer. And here one of the first of my great lessons as a writer began.

Up to this time I had been a young man who wanted to be a writer more than anything on earth and who had created his first book in the great blaze of illusion, hope, and wild desire which a young writer must feel when he has no evidence except his hope and wild desire to drive him on. Now, in a certain measure, this had changed. The hope had, to a small degree, been realized. The wild desire had, in a certain way, been attained. In brief, I had been a writer in hope and in desire before and now I was a writer in fact. My book had been published and read. It had had for a first book a good reception from the critics. It had had for a first book a good sale. My name was known and I was being talked about. I would read about myself, for example, as one of the "younger American writers." I was the person who, some of the critics said, was to be watched. They were looking forward to my future book with interest and with a certain amount of apprehension. Here, too, my education as a writer was increasing all the time. Now, indeed, I could read about myself and hear myself discussed as a young American writer, and somehow the fact was far more formidable than I had dreamed that it could be. I would read about my virtues and my defects as a writer and whether I showed promise of improving in the future or declining or whether I would ever produce another book — this honestly was a doubt that I had never considered but now these various reviews and criticisms began to eat and work into my consciousness — and the whole upshot of it was that I finally realized that my whole position as a writer had been changed. Before I had been a young, unknown man who wrote because he had to and who out of his dreaming and his desire invented his own visions of a publisher and a public and a bright fame such as he would like. Now, in a certain degree, I had these things but not in a way I had foreseen or even suspected. Now I was a young American writer, discussed and talked about, and I would read about myself and hear doubts and hopes expressed about my second book and my future work and get letters and advice and criticism from friends and strangers, some of which asked me in a friendly way if I could go on, if I had shot my bolt or not, if I thought I had any more to write about, if I was done for, finished, emptied out, or if the seeds of life were in me, if the power was in me which could make me keep producing.

My greatest worry at first was not one of doubt, mistrust, or lack of confidence in my own own power, but rather one of unforeseen and somehow terribly naked exposure. I had wanted fame, a book, a public, and a publisher as youth who ever wrote has wanted them, and now I had them. It was not the way I thought that it would be at all. It worried me, confused me, gave me a strange feeling of guilt and responsibility. I was a young American writer, and they had hopes and fears about my future, and what would I do, or would it be anything, nothing, much, or little? Would the faults which they had found in my work grow worse or would I conquer them? Was I another flash in the pan? Would I come through? What would happen to me?

I let it worry me. I would go home at night and look around my room and see that morning's coffee cup still unwashed and books on the floor and a shirt where I had thrown it the night before and great stacks of manuscript and everything so common and familiar looking and so disorderly, like all the rooms that we have ever lived in, and then I would think that I was now "a young American writer"; that somehow I was practicing an imposture on my readers and my critics because my shirt looked the way it did and my books and my bed—not, you understand, because they were disorderly, shabby, common, familiar, but just because they looked the way they did.

But now another fact began to gnaw away into my consciousness.

I was a young American writer; my first book had done well. The critics had begun to ask questions about the second one, and so now I had to think about the second one as well. I had always wanted to think about the second one and the thirty-second one and the fifty-second one. As an unknown and obscure boy who had wanted to write, I had been sure that I had a hundred books in me, that all of them would be good, that each of them would make me famous. But here again was a strange and jolting transition from wild hope and exultant conviction; and plain, blazing fact remained. As a young man who had wanted to write books and to be famous and to make writing the work of his life, and who had had nothing but this drunken hope of his own desire to cling to, the writing of fifty books had seemed easy. But now that I had actually written one and *they*, the actual readers and the critics who had read it, were looking for a second, I was up against it. I was not up against it the way I dreaded, not up against it in the way I feared to face, I was just up against it cold and hard as one comes up against a wall. I was a writer. I had made the writer's life my life; I had made the first step as a writer; it was the only step I could make; there was no going back; I had to go on. What could I do? After the first book there had to be a second book. What was the second book about? Whence did it come from?

This inexorable fact, although it became more and more pressing, did not bother me so much at first. Rather I was concerned with many other things that had to do with the publication of that first book, and as before, I had foreseen none of them. In the first place, I had not foreseen one fact which becomes absolutely plain and obvious after a man has written a book, but which he cannot foresee until he has written one. This fact is that we write a book not in order to remember it, but in order to forget it, and now having written the book, this fact was evident. As soon as the book was in print, I began to forget about it, I wanted to forget about it, I didn't want people to talk to me or question me about it. I became horribly embarrassed if they did talk to me about it or asked me what I meant by it in such and such a place and what my intentions were. I just wanted them to leave me alone and shut up about it. And yet, and here is a painful, intolerable enigma, the whole thing, I longed desperately for my book's good success. I wanted people, many people, to read it and admire it. I wanted them to think that I was a good writer. I wanted them to think that I had written a good book. I wanted my book to have the position of proud esteem and honor in the world that I longed for it to have—I wanted, in short, to be a successful and a famous man, and I wanted to lead the same kind of obscure and private life I'd always had and not to be told about my fame and success. I am sure it has been this way with every young man who ever wrote and hoped as I did.

From this perplexed and enigmatic problem, another painful and difficult situation was produced, for, having written, published and produced my book, I now began to feel this ghostly and remote detachment from it at the same time I was being faced daily with its living and fleshly presence in the world. People would write to me and talk to me about it, and I would try to answer, and I would feel like an imposter all the time. I would try to answer their questions, to tell them what I had meant when I had written such and such a scene, and all the time I was not only uncertain about what I had meant, but I found it impossible to recapture or make live again what I had felt and imagined when I had written the scene, and I would sometimes actually feel as if I had had nothing to do with it whatever. This, I think, is certainly one of the most painful and perplexing problems that a writer must face. It really seems that the reason a writer writes a book is to forget a book, and the reason a reader reads one is to remember it, and the conflict of these two premises produces at times a weird and incredible situation. I had, for example, written my first book more or less directly from the material and experience of my own life, and, furthermore, I now think that I may have written it with a certain harsh and

naked reality, a blazing directness which is likely to character-
ize the earliest work of a young and unskilled writer. At any
rate, I can honestly say that I did not foresee it. I foresaw none
of it. I was surprised not only by the kind of response my book
had with many of the critics and the general public, I was most
of all surprised with the response it had in my native town.

Although I had been apprehensive about certain things in
the book and a quality of naked directness which I have mentioned in reference to its effect upon the people in the town
where I was born, where most of my kinsmen and my relatives live, I had honestly not visioned the kind of effect the
book would have there. I had felt that a certain very limited
number of people would read it in my native town, that some
would like it, others be amused by it, and some indignant. I
was not prepared for what happened. I had thought there
might be a hundred people in that town who would read the
book, but if there are a hundred outside of the negro population, the blind, and the positively illiterate who have not read
it, I do not know where they are. For months the town seethed
and boiled with a fury of bitter excitement and passionate
resentment which I had not believed possible. The book and
the author were denounced from the pulpits by the ministers
of all the leading churches. Men collected on street corners to
debate, discuss, and generally denounce the book. For weeks
the women's clubs, bridge parties, teas, receptions, the whole
complex fabric of a small town's social life, was absorbed by an
outraged clamor. I received anonymous letters full of vilifica-
tion and abuse, one which threatened to kill me if I came back
home, others which were merely obscene. One venerable old
lady, whom I had known all my life, wrote me—in an extraordinary letter which ran to eight pages, which never stopped
once to draw a breath—that she wondered how I could have

such a crime upon my soul, and added that although she had never believed in lynch law, she would do nothing to prevent a mob from dragging that "big overgrown karkus" across the public square. She informed me further, that my mother had taken to her bed "as white as a ghost" and would "never rise from it again."

There were many other venomous and bitter attacks from my home town of this sort, and for the first time I learned another lesson which every young writer has got to learn. And that lesson is the naked, blazing power of print. It was, for me at that time, a bewildering and almost overwhelming situation, and I had not foreseen it. In the world outside I was beginning to win through my book a certain amount of reputation and critical esteem, and in my home town I had become practically an outlaw and a pariah. My elation and joy at the success my book had won was mixed with bitter chagrin and anxiety which the reception of my book in my native town was causing me. And yet I think I learned something from that situation, too; something that every young writer would consider an experience for himself. For the first time I was forced to consider squarely this problem: where does the material of an artist come from? What are the proper uses of that material, and how far must his freedom in the use of that material be controlled by his responsibility as a member of society? This is a terribly vexed and difficult problem, and I have by no means come to the bottom of it yet nor solved it to my own satisfaction. Perhaps I never will, but as a result of all the pain and apprehension which I suffered at that time and which others may have suffered on account of me as a result of that first book, I have done much thinking and arrived at certain conclusions.

My book was what is often referred to as an autobiographical novel. I protested against this term in a preface to the book upon the grounds that any serious work of creation is of necessity autobiographical and that few more autobiographical works than *Gulliver's Travels* have ever been written. I added that Dr. Johnson had remarked that a man might turn over all the volumes in his library to make a single book, and that in a similar way, a novelist might turn over half the characters in his native town to make a single figure for his novel. In spite of this—my argument that all creative work is autobiographical and that a man has got to use what is his own if what he does has value and he cannot use what is not his own, that a man must use somehow the materials of his own experience if what he does has value and he cannot use what are not the materials of his own experience—in spite of this, the people in my native town were not persuaded or appeased, and the charge of autobiography was brought against me in many other places.

I was quite indignant at that time because of this charge, but as time has gone on and I have had time to reflect on the very serious writing problem involved in this charge, my feeling is not so indignant or resentful as it once was. As I have said, my conviction is that all serious creative work must be at bottom autobiographical, and that a man must use the material and experience of his own life if he is to create anything that has substantial value. But I also believe now that the young writer is often led through inexperience to a use of the materials of life and memory which are, perhaps, somewhat too naked and direct for the purpose of a work of art. The thing a young writer, using his own life experience in this way, is likely to do is to confuse the limits between actuality and reality. He tends unconsciously to describe an event in such a way because it actually happened that way, and from an artistic point of view, I can now see that this is wrong. It is not, for example, important that one remembers a charming and beautiful woman of easy virtue as having come from the state of Kentucky in the year 1907. She could perfectly well have come from Idaho or Texas or Nova Scotia. The important thing really is only to express as well as possible that quality of the beautiful and charming woman of easy virtue. But the young writer, chained to fact and to his own inexperience, is yet unliberated by maturity, is likely to confuse actuality as necessity and to argue, "she must be described as coming from Kentucky because that is where she actually did come from."

In spite of this, it is literally impossible for a man who has the stuff of creation in him to make a literal transcription of his own experience. Everything in a work of art is changed and transfigured by the personality of the artist. And as far as my own first book is concerned, I can truthfully say that I do not believe that there is a single page of it that is true to fact. And from this circumstance, also, I learned another curious and wonderfully illuminating thing about writing. For although my book was not true to fact, it was true to the general experience of the town I came from and, I hope, of course, to the general experience of all men living. The best way I can describe the situation is this: it was as if I were a sculptor who had found a certain kind of clay with which to model. Now a farmer who knew well the neighborhood from which this clay had come might come by and find the sculptor at this work and say to him, "I know the farm from which you got that clay." But it would be unfair of him to say, "I know the figure, too." Now I think what happened in my native town is that having seen the clay, they became immediately convinced that they recognized the figure, too, and the results of this misconception were so painful and ludicrous that the telling of it is almost past belief. For example, I discovered for the first time—and here, too, is another discovery which every young writer must make—that once people you have known become convinced they recognize the material you have used, it is a very easy thing for them to become convinced that they recognize and remember every fact and incident that has gone into the making of your book.

It was my own experience to be assured by people from my native town not only that they remembered scenes and incidents and characters in my first book, which may have had some basis in actuality, but also that they remembered, and had even been present at, scenes and incidents in the book which so far as I know had no historical basis whatever. For example, there was one scene in the book in which a stonecutter is represented as selling to a notorious woman of the town the statue of a marble angel which he has treasured for many years. So far as I know, and, after all, I wrote the scene myself, there was no basis in fact or in story, and yet I was informed by several people later that they not only remembered the incident perfectly, but had actually been witnesses to the transaction. Nor was this the end of the story. The title of the book was *Look Homeward, Angel,* and the title comes from a line in the poem *Lycidas* by John Milton, the full sentence being: "Look homeward, Angel, now, and melt with ruth." This title proved extremely puzzling to people in my native town, and finally they concluded that the book derived its title from the stone angel previously mentioned on the stonecutter's porch, and that since this angel was facing in a general direction, consummate with the position of the stonecutter's home, the reason for the title *Look Homeward, Angel* became apparent. Following this logical conclusion, one of the newspapers sent one of its reporters and a photographer to the

cemetery where a photograph was taken of a large and imposing looking angel and printed in the paper with a statement to
the effect that the angel was the now famous angel which had
stood upon the stonecutter's porch for so many years and had
given the title to my book. The unfortunate part of this proceeding was that I had never seen or heard of this angel before,
and that this angel was, in fact, erected over the grave of a
well-known Methodist lady who had died a dew years before
and that her indignant family and relatives had immediately
written the paper to demand a retraction of its story, saying
that their mother had been in no way connected with the infamous book or the infamous angel which had given the infamous book its name. Such, then, were some of the unforeseen
problems and difficulties with which I was confronted after
the publication of my first book.

In my home town I was regarded as a black sheep, a pariah, and outcast who had cruelly and savagely attacked his
own people and had written a slanderous history of the com-
munity over the last fifty years. Elsewhere I was regarded on
the whole as a young writer of promise, a young man who
had written a first book which had been favorably received and
who was being watched by the critics with a certain amount
of hope and scepticism concerning his future work. My own
mind during those months was a seething caldron of joy, despair, hope, indignation, guilt, innocence, incertitude, and
passionate conviction. Having created and published one
book, that book had, of its own accord, created another life,
and now, having written that book, gotten it out of my system, feeling remote, detached and far away from it the way I
have described, I found myself suddenly plunged into the second life the book had of its own accord created.

I could not get away from it. I could not forget it. I was

eight hundred miles away from my native town, but in a way I lived and fought and sweat and struggled through the thousand different conflicts which my book was making there and at the same time I was living, struggling with a thousand other conflicts, speculations, questions which it had aroused elsewhere. In other words, I was living anew the life of the thing which I had finished. My life was being absorbed, possessed and dominated by the life of something to which I had given birth out of my own life and which I now wished to forget. And here again, I think, I learned for the first time something that every young writer has got to learn, something he cannot possibly know until it has happened to him. Here I was, a young man full of work, full of strength and power and hope and energy; and all this was being destroyed, consumed, eaten up by something I was done with, something I could do no more about, something my life should bother with no longer. What could I do? How could I get on with my work?

Month was passing into month. I had had a success. The way was opened to me. There was one thing for me to do and only one, and that was work, and I was spending my time consuming myself with anger, grief, regret and useless passion about the reception the book had had in my native town, about the thousand gossips, rumors, slanders, whisperings, situations it had created there, or wasting myself again in exultancy and joy because of the critics' and readers' praise, or in anguish and bitterness because of their dislike and ridicule. The nature of my conflict and my struggle hit me squarely between the eyes. For the first time, I realized the nature of one of the artist's greatest conflicts, and was faced with the need of meeting it. For the first time I saw not only that the artist must live and sweat and love and suffer and enjoy as other men, that he must know grief and death and danger and poverty and sorrow and all the hard and daily care of stern anxiety that other men must know, but that the artist must also work as other men and that furthermore, he must work and do as other men even while these things are going on. It seems a simple and banal assertion, but I learned it hardly, and in one of the hardest and worst moments of my life. There is no such thing as an artistic vacuum; there is no such thing as a time where the artist may work in a delightful and reposeful atmosphere, free of the sweat and anguish and agony that other men must know, or if the artist ever does find such a time, it is something not to be hoped for, something not to live for, something not to be sought for indefinitely. The artist must live and do and work through all the sweat and toil and grief and bitter, stern complexity of life in the same way that his father and every man that ever lived have had to do.

At any rate, while my life and time and energy were caught up and almost completely absorbed in the emotional vortex which my first book had created, I was getting almost no work done on the second. In fact, during all this time, save for a great many notes, fragments, snatches of dialogue and character which I wrote down in the big ledgers in which I did my writing, I made no serious and sustained effort at composition whatever. And now I was faced with another grave and fundamental problem which every young beginning writer must meet squarely if he is to continue. How is a man to get his writing done? How long should he work at writing, and how often? What kind of method, if any, must he find in following his work? I suddenly found myself face to face with the grim necessity of steady, constant, daily work. And as simple as this discovery may seem to all of you, I was not prepared for it.

In a way, you see, my status had changed almost overnight from the status of an amateur—may I say a kind of inspired amateur who wrote from the exuberance of wild hope and a necessity to express himself but who, like every unfledged writer who has not been published, was shooting in the dark toward a shining but uncertain goal—my status had changed then, I say, from this capacity to that of a man who had, to a certain degree, established himself, found a reading public which was interested in what he did and who was expected to continue. Now it had never occurred to me in my amateur days that I would not continue. I had every intention, every conviction of continuing, but the practical and immediate necessity of continuing had not been evident then as it was now. A young man writing his first book, a young writer without a publisher and a public, does not feel the sense of necessity, the pressure of time, as does a writer who has been published and who must now begin to think of time schedules, publishing seasons, and the completion of his next book. I realized suddenly with a sense of definite shock that I had let six months go by since the publication of my first book and that, save for the notes and fragments I have mentioned, I had done nothing.

Meanwhile the book continued to sell slowly but steadily, and in February, 1930, about five months after its publication, I found it possible to resign from the faculty of New York University, where I was employed as an instructor in English at the Washington Square College, and devote my full time to the preparation of a second book. I was also fortunate enough to be awarded the Guggenheim Fellowship that spring which would enable me to live and work abroad for a year. And accordingly at the beginning of May, I went abroad again.

I was in Paris for a couple of months until the middle of June, and although I now began to work more earnestly and compelled myself to work for four or five hours a day, my effort at composition was still confused, broken, and unconsecutive, and although isolated chapters, scenes, and sections did begin to emerge now, there was nothing yet that had the structural form and unity of a book. Moreover, the life of Paris, which I have always found a curious mixture of strong excitement and indolent languor, disturbed me. The life of the great city fascinated me as it had always done, but also aroused all the old feelings of naked homelessness, rootlessness, and loneliness which I have always felt there. It was, and has always remained for me, at least, the most homesick city in the world; the place where I have felt mostly an alien and a stranger, and certainly for me as fascinating and seductive as the city is, it has never been a good place to work. But here I would like to say something about places to work because that is another problem which causes young writers a great deal of doubt, uncertainty, and confusion, and I think, uselessly.

I had gone through the whole experience and now I was almost done with it. I had come to Paris first six years before, a youth of 24, filled with all the romantic faith and foolishness which many young men at that time felt when they saw Paris. I had come there that first time, so I told myself, to work, and so strong and glamorous was the magic name of Paris, the fascination it exerted over our imaginations at that time, that I really thought one could work far better in Paris than anywhere on earth; that it was a place where the very air was impregnated with the energies of art; where the artist was bound to find a more fortunate and happy life than he could possibly find in America. Now I had come to see that this was all wrong. I had come to understand very plainly that what many of us were doing in those years when we fled from our own country and sought refuge abroad was not really looking for a place to work, but looking for a place where we could escape from work; that what we were really fleeing from in those years was not the Philistinism, the materialism, and ugliness in American life which we said we were fleeing from, but from the necessity of grappling squarely with ourselves and the stern and bitter necessity of finding in ourselves, somehow, the stuff to live by, to get from our own lives and our own experience the substance and material of our art which every man who ever lived and wrote a living thing has had to get out of himself and without which he is lost.

Now I remembered how many of us, young men I had known at Harvard in the playwriting class, or in the South, or in New York, young men who wanted to paint or write or compose music or thought they wanted to do these things, had come to Paris because it was the place to work and then had gone to Spain because they thought they could work better there, and then had gone to Italy, or Majorca or Capri or to some other place, and always because it was the place where they could work. And then I remembered how little had come of it, how pitifully little; how little work we had done, and how we had lied to ourselves and deceived ourselves. Thus I learned finally and forever what I hope no one here will ever have to learn at all, another simple, fundamental and perhaps banal lesson, an error which may not, I hope, trouble young writers of the present day so much, but which was deeply rooted in the lives of many young people at that time and which brought utter ruin to some of them and a great and needless confusion, waste, and suffering to others. I learned finally and forever the truth in the great utterance of the poet, Horace: "You can change your skies, but not your soul," and

I saw suddenly that what many of us had been doing for years had been to change our skies constantly in the hope that by such change some magic transformation would be wrought in our own spirit; that what we had really been doing all this time when we had been going to Paris, Spain, and Italy to work was really to seek an escape, to fly from the stern necessity of conflict and of labor, somehow to get away from the indolence, the lack of substance, power, courage or talent in our own spirits. I learned instantly and forever that this mythical, this magical, this wonder-working, miraculous, and mysterious place to work was everywhere, was all around us, was wherever we happened to be so long as the power, the will, the overwhelming and inexorable necessity to work was in ourselves.

The place to work! Yes, the place to work *was* Paris; it *was* Spain; it *was* Italy and Capri and Majorca, but great God, it was also Keokuk, and Portland, Maine, and Denver, Colorado, and Yancey County, North Carolina, and wherever we might be if work was there within us at the time; and yet if this was all that I had learned from all these voyages to Europe, if the price of all this wandering had been just this simple lesson, it would have been worth the price, but that was not all. I had found out during all these years of wandering that the way to discover one's own country was to leave it; that the way to find America was to find it in one's heart, one's mind, one's memory, and one's spirit, and in a foreign land. So had it been with me. Around me day by day in all these months and years and voyages to Europe I had seen the million forms and shapes and patterns of an alien life. My life had been enriched and quickened immeasurably by contemplating and experiencing them, and always when I saw them I had the profit of a vast, fertile, inestimable comparison. All of my powers of memory and experience were constantly brought to bear as I compared the life of which I was a part, the country from which I came, with this new and alien life in which I lived and wandered as a stranger.

I think I may say that I discovered America during these years abroad out of my very need of her. I found her because I had left her. The huge gain of this discovery seemed to come directly from my sense of loss. I had been to Europe five times now; each time I had come with longing, delight, with maddening eagerness to return, and each time how, where, and in what way I did not know, I had felt the bitter ache of homelessness, a desperate need and longing for America, an overwhelming desire to return.

Now during that summer in Paris, I think I felt this great homesickness more than ever before, and I really believe that from this emotion, this constant and almost intolerable effort of memory and desire, this thing that would not let me rest, this memory of home that could not be appeased, that would not stop or vanish even when I slept—from this huge and hopeless memory of home, I say, I think the material and the structure of the books I now began to write were derived.

Perhaps some of you have expected a talk of a more practical and technical nature concerning the elements of writing, and perhaps it may have seemed to you that up to now I have really talked more about the spiritual and emotional difficulties that confront a young writer than about the practical aspects of his work and his profession, but I assure you that I am a tremendously concrete and practical person where writing is concerned, and that what I have been doing thus far has been just to prepare the way for a description of the whole physical problem, the practical and concrete elements of the work which was to occupy all my time for the next four and a half years. I have, for example, a very tenacious, a very literal, vivid, concrete memory. The quality of my memory is characterized, I believe, in a more than ordinary degree by the intensity of its sense impressions, its power to evoke and bring back the odors, sounds, colors, shapes, and feel of things with concrete vividness. Now my memory was at work night and day in a way that I could at first neither check nor control and that swarmed unbidden at all hours and moments of the day and night in a stream of blazing pageantry across my mind with the million forms and substances of the life and air that I had left, from which I had been derived, which was my own, America.

The astonishing variety, exactness and profusion of these images may seem grotesque and comical to you, and yet they came unbidden; they filled my life, my mind, my waking and my sleeping hours. I could not have prevented them even if I had tried. And what were they? It was not merely the images of a larger and more general kind, I mean such images as the wild and casual look of the American landscape when contrasted with the suave, controlled, and fertile cultivation of Europe. It was not merely the sense of lavish space and continental distance which inhabits the spirit of the American and which returns to him with overwhelming force when he first experiences the sense of confinement, the small-fenced geographies of Europe. It was not merely these larger and more obvious aspects of America in contrast to the European scene, but it was a million smaller and more poignant things as well. I would be sitting, for example, on the terrace of a café watching the flash and play of life before me on the Avenue de l'Opéra and suddenly I would remember the iron railing that goes along the boardwalk at Atlantic City. I could see it instantly just the way it was, the heavy iron pipe; its raw, galvanized look; the way the joints fitted together. It was all so vivid and concrete that I could feel my hand upon it and know the exact dimensions, its size and weight and shape. And suddenly with a flash of blinding discovery, I would realize that I had never seen any railing that looked like this in Europe. And this utterly familiar, common, and perhaps ugly thing would suddenly be revealed to me with all the strangeness and wonder with which we discover a thing which we have seen and lived with all our lives and yet have never known before.

Or again, it would be a bridge, the look of an old iron bridge across an American river, the sound the train makes as it goes across it; the spoke and hollow rumble of the ties below; the look of the muddy banks; the slow, thick, yellow wash of an American river; an old flat-bottomed boat half filled with water stogged in the muddy bank; or it would be, most lonely and haunting of all the sounds I know, the sound of a milk wagon as it entered an American street just at the first gray of the morning, the slow and lonely clopping of the hoof upon the street, the jink of bottles, the sudden rattle of a battered old milk can, the swift and hurried footsteps of the milkman, and again the jink of bottles, a low word spoken in silence to his horse, and then the great, slow, clopping hoof receding into silence, and then quietness and a bird song rising in the street again.

Or it would be a little wooden shed out in the country two miles from my home town where people waited for the street car, and I could see and feel again the dull and rusty color of the old green paint and see and feel all of the initials that had been carved out with jackknives on the planks and benches within the shed, and smell the warm and sultry smell so resinous and so thrilling, so filled with a strange and nameless excitement of an unknown joy, a coming prophecy, and hear the street car as it came to a stop, the moment of brooding, drowsing silence; a hot thrum and drowsy stitch at three o'clock; the smell of grass and hot sweet clover; and then the sudden sense of absence, loneliness and departure when the street car had gone and there was nothing but the hot drowsy stitch at three o'clock again.

Or again, it would be a city street, an American street with all its jumble of a thousand gaunt, confused, and harshly ugly architectures. It would be Montague Street or Fulton Street in Brooklyn, or Eleventh Street in New York, or other streets where I had lived; and suddenly I would see a gaunt and harsh and savage webbing of the elevated structure along Fulton Street, and how the lights swarmed through in dusty, broken bars, and I could remember the old, familiar rusty color, that incomparable rusty color that gets into so many things here in America, and this also would be like something I had seen a million times and lived with all my life. It was familiar to me as my mother's face, and yet it would seem to me now that I had never really known it; that I had just discovered it; that I had never found a name for it, a tongue to give it utterance.

I would sit there, looking out upon the Avenue de l'Opéra and my life would ache with the whole memory of it; the desire to see it again; somehow to find a word for it; a language that would tell its shape, its color, the way we have all known and felt and seen it. And it was the same with a million other things as well—the look of a string of empty freight cars standing on a track; the shape and look and weight of the rails; the look of the rock ballast; the old, dried, blood-coloring of the empty string of freight cars; the floor of a freight car silted over with white flour; the strange and haunting thrill that is somehow like strong joy and sorrow and loneliness when we see a string of empty freights curving away along a spur of rusty track in panland barrens somewhere in America; at the red and ragged flame of sunset and raw wintery March.

It would be all these things and a million other things as well of which there is no time here to describe—a stone, a leaf, a blade of grass, the bark of a tree, the rusty door and window frames of old rusty-looking shops in Fulton Street, the sugar maple flaming into bitter red in Vermont at the beginning of October, the majesty, power, and comfort of the great red barns of Pennsylvania; the sweep and undulance of the bronze, red earth; the apple orchards in the glory of their still, dense bloom incredible; the stiff, clean rustling of the corn blades at night; their sweet, clean smell as one passes them in a racing motor car; the look of a tree smashed down and fallen across the clean and rock-like clamor of a boiling mountain stream in western North Carolina; the sound of the engines shifting in the freight yards in my native town at night; the acrid, faintly smoky smell of the Hudson Tube; the old worn smell of the wood of baseball bleachers in July when the game is over, and the sight of the men in shirtsleeves screaming, flowing, reeling out across the field; the look and smell of the ferry house and the ferry slips and all of the morning faces packed and turned like petals in a bow towards Manhattan. These and a million other things which all of us have known, which all of us remember, which are the breath, the blood, the substance of our lives, but now came back to me in a blazing imagery, in a torrential flood tide of aching and intolerable memory, and suddenly I understood clearly for the first time in my life that I had no language for them, no words to give them utterance, no tongue to tell their shape, dimension, tone, and special quality, and all the meaning and emotion that they have for us. And when I saw and understood this thing, I saw that I must find a language for myself, find for myself the tongue to utter what I knew but could not say. And from the day and moment of that discovery, the line and purpose of my life was shaped. The end toward which every energy of my life and talent would be henceforth directed was in such a way as this defined.

This was certainly a discovery of major importance so far as my future development as a writer was concerned, but so far as the immediate task before me was concerned, the writing of the next book, the discovery was very far from being a final or definitive one. I had made a discovery, which was to shape the purpose of my life for several years, which had shown me the vast problem of articulation that lay before me, which, in a sense, revealed a whole new world to me, but at that moment it seemed to give me very little help toward defining and determining my book. Rather it was as if I had discovered a whole new universe of chemical elements and had begun to see certain relations between some of them but had by no means begun to organize and arrange the whole series in such a way that they would crystallize into a harmonious and coherent union. From this time on, I think my effort might be described as the effort to complete that organization, to discover that articulation for which I strove, to bring about that final coherent union. I have not yet succeeded in doing so, but I feel that I am on my way. I know that I have failed thus far in doing so, but I believe I understand pretty thoroughly just where the nature of my failure lies, and of course my deepest and most earnest hope is that the time will come when I will not fail.

At any rate, from this time on the general progress of the three books which I was to write in the next four and a half years could be fairly described in somewhat this way. It was a progress that began in a whirling vortex and a creative chaos and that proceeded slowly at the expense of infinite confusion, toil, and error toward clarification and the articulation of an ordered and formal structure. My editor, who worked and strove and suffered with me through the greater part of this period, shrewdly and humorously likened the making of these books to the creation of the world as described in Genesis: "In the beginning God created the heaven and the earth. 2. And the earth was without form, and void; and darkness *was* upon the face of the deep. And the Spirit of God moved upon the face of the waters."

An extraordinary image remains to me from that year, the year I spent abroad, when the material and the design of these books first began to take on an articulate form. I had been for several months aware that all the material of the book was in me; that it had, somehow, to find release and the design of a coherent structure, but at that time I did not know, I could not discover what design and what structure the book must take. The image that came to me at that time and that represented the state of my creative consciousness more accurately and truly than any other was this: It seemed that I had inside me, swelling and gathering in power and weight and menace all the time, a huge black cloud, and that this cloud was electric, the menace of a coming storm; that it was loaded with a kind of hurricane violence that could not be held in check much longer; that this storm was gathering all the time; that the very air was pregnant with its brooding hush; that the moment was approaching fast when it must break. Well, all I can tell you is that the storm did break. It broke that summer while I was in Switzerland. It came in torrents, and it is not over yet.

I cannot really say the book was written. It was not constructed word by word or line by line or chapter by chapter. It came from me like lava pouring from the crater of a volcano. It was constructed on a scale in which the words were reckoned not by thousands, but by millions. It was something that took hold of me and possessed me, and before I was done with it—that is before I finally emerged with the first completed part—it seemed to me that it had done for me. The tenement of one man's heart and brain and flesh and bone and sinew, the little vessel of his one life, could not possibly endure, could not possibly be strong enough or big enough to hold this raging tempest of his creative need.

The book began to come that year while I was abroad, but it began to come at first without form, without structure, without any narrative plan or sequence whatever. It was exactly as if this great black storm cloud I have spoken of had opened up and, 'mid flashes of lightning, was pouring from its depth a torrential and ungovernable flood. Upon that flood everything was swept and borne along like a great river in the South in its flood tide of the spring, and I was borne along with it. I wrote because this floodtide power of writing had flowed through me and swept me with it, and I could not do otherwise. During that first period all that I can now say is that the writing wrote itself.

And what did I write about? What was this floodtide river of creation which swept me with it in its rolling and ungovernable tide? It was no planned nor plotted scheme of life, no ordered narrative, no planned design. There was nothing at first which could be called a novel. I wrote about night and darkness in America and the huge coming out of sleep, and the faces of the sleepers in ten thousand little towns; and of the tides of sleep and how the rivers flowed forever in the darkness. I wrote about the hissing glut of tides upon the thousand miles of coast; of how the moonlight blazed down on the wilderness and filled the cat's cold eye with blazing yellow. I wrote about death and sleep, and of that enfabled rock of life we call the city. I wrote about October, of great trains that thundered through the night, of ships and stations in the morning; of men in harbors and traffic of the ships.

I spent the winter of that year in England from October until March, and here during this period, perhaps because of the homely familiarity of the English life, the sense of order and repose which such a life can give you, my work moved forward still another step from this floodtide chaos of creation. I began to get control, to shape and govern consciously its huge materials. For the first time the work began to take on the lineaments of design. These lineaments were still confused and broken, sometimes utterly lost, but now I really did get the sense at last that I was working on a great block of marble, shaping a figure which no one but its maker could as yet define, but which was emerging more and more into the sinewy lines of composition. My design for the book was growing firmer every day; my plan surer and more precise.

From the beginning — and this was one fact that in all my times of hopelessness and doubt returned to fortify my faith in my conviction — the idea, the central legend that I wished my book to express had not changed. And this legend, this central idea which I wanted my book in all its various ways to illustrate and which I hoped would always be present either in fact or by implication was this: the deepest search in life, it seemed to me, the fundamental adventure, the thing that in one way or another was central to all living was man's search to find a father, not merely the father of his life and flesh, not merely the lost father of his youth, but the image of a strength and wisdom external to his need and superior to his hunger, to which the belief and power of his own life could be united.

Yet I was terribly far away from the actual accomplishment of a book—how far away I could not at that time foresee. But four more years would have to pass before the first of the series of books on which I was now embarked would be ready for the press, and if I could have known at that time what lay before me in those next four years; if I could have known how four years could lengthen, widen out into an ocean depth of time and memory; if I could have known that in those next four years there would be packed a century of living, a hundred lives of birth and death, despair, defeat, and triumph and the sheer exhaustion of a brute fatigue; if I had really known all that lay before me in the next four years, I do not know whether or not I could have found the power within myself to continue. But I was still sustained by the exuberant optimism of youth. My temperament, which is pessimistic about many things, has always been a curiously sanguine one concerning time, and although more than a year had now gone by and I had done no more than write great chants on death and sleep, prepare countless notes and trace here and there the first dim outlines of a formal pattern, I was confident that by the spring or the fall of the next year my book would somehow miraculously be ready. And yet what I had so far was not so much the ordered plan of a book—indeed I had no ordered plan at all —as a kind of jammed conception, the idea of man's constant search through life to find his father, and this, of course, was not itself a plan so much as it was an idea from which a legend that might produce one book or a great number of books perhaps could be derived.

It is true that during all of this time I had a general conception of what my book would be about. It would be called *The October Fair*—that title had already been announced by the publishers—and although I had not yet found, save in the most imperfect and uncertain way, the design that book would follow, I had a very good notion, a very full and complete understanding of what that book would be about. In other words, I knew what was going to be in the book. The critics, I suppose, might say that I had too full and complete an understanding, and that my real difficulty was not in knowing what was going to be in the book, but in not knowing what ought to be out of the book.

At any rate, so far as I can describe with any accuracy, the progress of that winter's work in England, the most definite progress towards the accomplishment of the book, was not along the lines of planned design and formal structure, but along this line that I have mentioned—writing some of the things, some of the chapters, incidents, and sections which I knew would have to be in the book. Meanwhile what was really going on in my mind, in my whole creative consciousness, during all this time, although I did not realize it at the moment, was this: What I was really doing, what I had been doing all this time since my discovery of my America in Paris the summer before, was really to explore day by day and month by month with a fanatical intensity, a devoted thoroughness that would make the most patient and minute researches of German scholarship seem superficial by comparison, the whole material domain of my resources as a man and as a writer. This exploration went on in this intensive way for a period which I can estimate conservatively as two years and a half. It is still going on, although not with the same all-absorbing and fanatical intensity, because the work it led to, the work that after infinite toil and waste and labor it helped me wonderfully to define and shape, that work has reached such a state of final definition and completion that the immediate task of finishing it is the one that now occupies the energy and interest of my life.

Because of that intense and all-consuming research, I think that the publication of my next book was set back at least two, and perhaps three, years. Because of it, I wasted countless hours and days and months of labor; wrote hundreds of thousands of words that could not be used; was led off and betrayed into innumerable blind alleys; tempted by the enchanting prospect of grand and magic vistas which this whole labor of exploration was opening up before me constantly, but which led me away constantly from the work I had at hand, the job that I must finish. And yet, as wasteful, as full of confusion and error, as mistaken as much of this exploration was, I think that I would have to consider it as a most valuable experience I have yet had as a writer.

It is true that it is something I did not do so much with deliberate intent as something which took hold of me and would not let me go until it had finished with me and I with it. In a way, during that period of my life, I think I was like the Ancient Mariner who told the Wedding Guest that his frame was wrenched by the woeful agony which forced him to begin his tale before it left him free. In my own experience, my wedding guests were the great ledgers in which I wrote, and the tale which I told to them would have seemed, I am afraid, completely incoherent, as meaningless as Chinese characters, had any reader seen them. What then were some of the practical aspects of this research, this exploration that I have mentioned which had begun in Paris the summer before and which now was continuing day by day along with the actual work of composition which I have mentioned? What were some of the things which I put down in these enormous ledgers, filling book after book in this furious attempt to define the physical limits of my experience?

Well, I will try to tell you a little of it in the hope that you may get some general idea of the whole. I could by no means hope to give you a comprehensive idea of its whole extent because three years of work and perhaps a million and a half words went into these books. It included everything from gigantic and staggering lists of the towns, cities, counties, states, and countries I had been in, to minutely thorough, desperately evocative descriptions of the undercarriage, the springs, wheels, flanges, axelrods, color, weight, and quality of the day coach of an American railway train. One could open these huge ledgers at random and find whole sections devoted to such topics as this: How many towns have I known with a population of twenty-five thousand or more? How many of these towns do I know especially well to write something about them, and in how many of these towns have I had some experience either of observation, emotion, or living contact such as would give me some vital creative connection with the life of the town? And then there would be other lists of the towns under twenty-five thousand and the towns under three thousand; lists of the counties and states of America of which I had some living and practical knowledge, and lists of those of which I had none. There would be similar lists for the cities, towns, and countries in Europe with which I had a similar connection, and lists of those with which I had none. There would be lists of the rooms and houses, hotel rooms, lodging house rooms, rooms in private dwellings, rooms in far farm houses, and rooms in city flats in which I had lived or in which I had slept for at least a night together with the most accurate and evocative descriptions of those rooms that I could write—their size, their shape, the color and design of the wall-paper, the way a towel hung down, the way a chair creaked, a streak of water rust upon the ceiling. There were countless charts, catalogs, descriptions that I can only classify here under the general heading of Amount and Number. What were the total combined populations of all the countries in Europe and America? In how many of those countries had I had some personal and vital experience? To what extent could one man have a comprehensive knowledge of a whole nation? In the course of my twenty-nine or thirty years of living, seeing, feeling, and experiencing, how many people had I seen? How many had I passed by on the streets? How many had I looked at? How many had I seen on trains and subways, in theatres, at baseball or football games? In the four or five years in which I had lived in New York, how many of its total population of seven or eight millions had I seen and passed and known in this way? How many had I actually come to know by name? With how many had I actually had some vital and illuminating experience, whether of joy, pain, anger, pity, love, reverence, respect, or simple, casual companionship however brief?

In addition to these great charts and catalogs and descriptive passages of cities, people, towns, states, and countries that I had known well, one might come upon other sections under some such cryptic heading as "Where now?" Under such a heading as this, there would be brief and flash-like notations of those hundreds and thousands of things which all of us have seen for just a flash, a moment in our lives which are lost, gone, vanished to never be recaptured even at the moment that we see them, which seem to be trivial, fleeting, of no consequence whatever at the moment that we see them and which are in our minds and hearts forever, which we can never forget, whose importance and significance we cannot attempt to estimate since practically they seem to have no importance and significance at all, but which are somehow pregnant with all the joy and sorrow of the human destiny, the tragic briefness of man's days, and which we know, somehow, are therefore more important than many things of more apparent consequence. "Where now?" Some quiet steps that came and passed along a leafy night-time street in summer in a little town down South long years ago; the voices quiet and low and casual strangely near, familiar, suddenly as they pass the house in darkness; a woman's voice, her sudden burst of low and tender laughter; then the voices and the footsteps going, silence, the leafy rustle of the trees; a motor car far away across the night; a screen door slammed, silence, darkness, once again? "Where now?" Two trains that met and paused at a little station, who knows where, at some little town at some unknown moment upon the huge breast and body of the continent; a girl who looked and smiled from the window of the other train; another passing in a motor car on the streets of Norfolk; the winter boarders in a little boarding house down South twenty years ago; Miss Florrie Mangle, the trained nurse; Miss Jessie Flenner, the cashier at Smith's drug store; Dr. Richards, the clairvoyant; the girl who cracked the whip and thrust her head into the lion's mouth with a Johnny J. Jones Carnival; Mr. Hoffman, the drunken and mild-mannered little stonecutter who worked for my father and told fabulous stories about hand-to-hand combats with man-eating sharks; the one-armed nigger who drove a wagon for the Carolina Coal and Ice Company; the wonderful way he handled his team with one good arm, backed the wagon up the alleyway, shoveled the coal into the cellar with a huge and shining pitchfork, all done without confusion, waste, or error and with one good arm; a boy named Victor Roncey whom I hated just because he had pompous, bulging piano legs, a dark face with a mole above his upper lip and a dark, sneering arrogant way of looking at people; another boy named Nebraska Redmond who was a wonderful boy, a plain, gentle, countrified kind of boy as brave as a lion and good at everything — hunting, swimming, wrestling, playing baseball — and for that reason, I felt, so much like his wonderful name, Nebraska, that I could never think of him as possibly having any other name.

"Where now?" It went beyond the limits of man's actual memory. It went back to the farthest adyt of his childhood before conscious memory had begun, the way he thought he must have felt the sun one day and heard Peagram's cow next door wrenching the coarse grass against the fence, or heard the street car stop upon the hill above his father's house at noon; and Earnest Peagram coming home to lunch, his hearty voice in midday greeting; and then the street car going and an iron gate slamming, and then the light of that lost day fades out. He can recall no more and does not know if what he has recalled is fact or fable or a fusion of the two. Where now — in these great ledger books, month after month, I wrote such things as this. Not only the concrete, material record of man's ordered memory, the things he knew that he had seen, the places gone to and the persons known, but all the things he scarcely dares to think he has remembered; all the flicks and darts and haunting lights that flash across the ancient and swarm-haunted mind of man that will return unbidden at an unexpected moment; a voice once heard; an eye that looked; a mouth that smiled; a face that vanished; the way the sunlight came and went; the rustling of a leaf upon a bough; a stone, a leaf, a door.

It may be objected, it has been objected already by certain

---

critics who have written about the work that I have thus far published, that in such research, such exploration as I have here attempted to describe there is a quality of intemperate excess, uncontrolled inclusiveness, an almost insane hunger to devour the entire body of human experience, to attempt to include more, pile in more, experience more than the measure of one life can hold or than the limits of a single work of art can well define. I freely and readily admit the validity and truth of this criticism. I admit that such hunger as I have here indicated may pass beyond the limits of sanity and reason. I admit further that this excess of preoccupation with the elements of amount and number, this torturing conflict of man against the mass, of the one and the many, this struggle with the huge and swarming web of human life, with the million complex forms of human experience has tormented me since my twentieth year and has driven me to unreasonable excesses in a hopeless attempt to read all the books, to know all the people, to see all the countries in the world—in short, to eat the world and have it too. I think I realize as well as anyone the fatal dangers that are consequent to such a ravenous desire, the damage it may wreak upon one's life and on one's work. But having had this thing within me, it was in no way possible for me to reason it out of me, no matter how cogently and clearly my reason worked against it. The only way I could meet it was to meet it squarely, not with reason but with life.

I had it in me; it was part of my life; for many years it was my life; and the only way I could get it out of me was to live it out of me, and that is what I did. I have not wholly succeeded in that purpose yet, but I have succeeded better than I at one time dared to hope. And I now not only understand, I really believe and know that so far as the artist is concerned, the unlimited spread and extent of human experience is not so important for him as the depth and intensity with which he experiences things. I also know with my life now—and, believe me, for the artist that is the only way to know anything —it is good to know things with one's head, but we cannot live and create with the things which we know with our head only. I say I know with my life now what I before only knew with my head, and that is that it is a great deal more important to have known one hundred living men and women in New York, to have understood their lives, to have got, somehow, at the root and source from which their lives and natures came than to have seen or passed or talked with seven million people upon the city streets.

And what finally I should most like to say to all of you about this research, this exploration which absorbed my life for years and which I have attempted to describe is this: That foolish and mistaken as much of it may seem to you, as excessive, monstrous, and intemperate, even useless as some of these great charts and catalogs which I have mentioned may seem to you, the total quality, end, and impact of that whole experience was not useless, monstrous or excessive. And from my own point of view, at least, it is in its whole implication the one practical thing I may have to tell you as a writer which may be of some concrete value to you. What I am trying to say to you here and now is this: When it was suggested to me that I come out here and talk to you, your director also suggested that the subject I might talk to you about was the "Making of a Book." I wrote and told him the subject suited me splendidly. I explained to him that I was not a skilled, professional writer, and I asked him if he did not think it was far better if I came out here and tried to tell you without equivocation or pretense just what kind of experience one man had actually had in the making of a book—what his blunders were, how he had failed or how succeeded, describe so far as he was able the whole course of experiment, research, trial, error, failure, and fulfillment and all its various and progressive stages so far as he could remember them.

That is what I have attempted to do. And as regards this long process of research and exploration which I have described, while I would by no means defend the process in its entirety, while I would freely admit that the process took hold of me at first instead of my taking hold of it, while I would earnestly and fervently hope that none of you would fall into the same errors of intemperate and unreasonable excess that characterized so much of my own research, I do want to say that I consider this experience on the whole the most valuable and practical in my whole experience thus far as a writer. I should also like to say that with all the waste and error and confusion it led me into, the innumerable and blind alleys, it brought me closer to a concrete definition of my resources, a true estimate of my energies and talents at this period of my life, and, most of all, toward a rudimentary, a just-beginning, but a living apprehension of the articulation I am looking for, the speech I must discover for myself, the tongue, the language I have got to have if, as an artist, my life is to proceed and grow, than any other thing that has ever happened to me.

I know the door is not yet open. I know the tongue, the speech, the language that I seek is not yet found, but I believe with all my heart that I have found the way, have made a channel, am started on my first beginning. And I believe with all my heart, also, that each man for himself and in his own way, each man who ever hopes to make a living thing out of the power and substance of his one life, must find that way, that speech, that tongue, that language, and that door—must find it for himself as I have tried to do. And that is why I have spoken to you as I have tonight.

And finally — this is the last I shall say about this experience, which I have called an experience of research and exploration — finally I should like to say that with all the waste and error that it caused me, with all the useless and extravagant excess that characterized my own effort, I think it is far better for a writer to go through such and experience, to explore first so far as he can his own resources, limits, and capacities, as a man and as an artist, than to attend somebody's school for how to write plays or stories or to try to get from books of technique or from books of other writers the line, the form, the pattern and design he should get for himself. I suppose all of us are familiar with Robert Louis Stevenson's celebrated description of his own apprenticeship. He played, he said, "this sedulous ape" to the works of many writers. He absorbed their style, their method and technique so that he could imitate any of them, and he concluded that this was the way to write, the inescapable way, the only way no matter what any man might say to the contrary. Well, I am saying to the contrary. I think that he was wrong, gifted, charming, talented story-teller that he was, and I think that in his utterance may also be found the basic error, the invalidity of his own work. This, of course, is a matter of opinion and highly arguable, but this is my own position.

SUCH, THEN, were the long, confused and painful beginnings of the book. When I returned to America early in the spring of 1931, the chief results of my year abroad might be summarized as follows: I had discovered, if not a plan or a design for the structure of my book, a kind of method of research, a sort of illumination which indicated to me the extent and potential value of my material even if it had not succeeded in effecting a structural articulation that could give a single work the unity of planned design. Furthermore, I had begun to mark out and define a few of the actual incidents and sections in the narrative, and had actually written some of them. Finally, I brought back with me three or four hundred thousand words of writing, some of it lyrical and poetic, such as the sections about sleep and death and October and the River which I have mentioned—and if I may say so, the weather, the temper of the book rather than its narrative and sequential body, and a great deal of its extensive and multitudinous notes along the lines of research I have previously described.

Thus, when I returned to America in March of that year, although I had three or four hundred thousand words of such material, I had as yet nothing that could be published as a novel. Almost a year and a half had elapsed since the publication of my first book and already people—my friends and acquaintances, people who had read my first book, and some of the critics—had begun to ask that question which is so well meant, so apparently harmless, so natural, but which as year followed year was to become more hateful and intolerable to my ears than the most malicious and deliberate mockery or insult could have been: "Have you finished your next book yet?" "When is it going to be published?"

At this time, on my return from Europe in 1931, although I realized the nature of my difficulty and knew I had nothing ready to be published as a book, my spirit was still immensely hopeful and confident, and I was sure that a few months of hard and steady work would bring the book to completion. I lost no time in getting established and starting to work. I found a place, a little basement flat in a little brick house in an alleyway in the Assyrian quarter in South Brooklyn, partly from reasons of economy and partly because I was sure that the isolation and remoteness of the place, so far at least as literary Manhattan was concerned, should be conducive to hard labor, and there I went about my task again.

The spring passed into the summer; the summer, into autumn. I was working hard and steadily, day after day, and still nothing that had the unity and design of a single work appeared. October came and with it a second full year since the publication of my first book. And now, for the first time, as that publishing season came and passed, I was lost irrevocably so far as the publication of my book was concerned. I began to feel the sensation of pressure, doubt, and naked desperation, which was to become more and more frequent, which finally would become almost maddeningly intolerable in the next three years. But during all this time, I was really making another long step forward toward the realization of my project. For the first time during the spring, summer, and autumn of that year I began to get some clear and coherent picture of the real extent and measure of my plan. For the first time I began to realize that my project was much larger than I had though it was. I had still believed, or had made myself believe at the time of my return from Europe, that I was writing a single book, that the title of that book would be *The October Fair*, and that the book, although large, would be comprised within the limits of about two hundred thousand words. Now as scene followed scene, as character after character came into being, as my investigation and understanding of my material became clearer and more comprehensive, I discovered that it would be impossible to write the book I had planned within the limits I had at first thought would be sufficient.

All of this time I was struggling, was being baffled by a

certain time element in the book, by a time relation which was inherent in the material and which could not be escaped, and for which I was now desperately, and, it seemed, fruitlessly, seeking some structural channel. Briefly, what I now discovered about my material as my knowledge of its extent and quality became more acute and comprehensive was this: There were three time elements inherent in the material. The first and most obvious was an element of actual present time, an element which carried the narrative forward, which represented characters and events as living in the present time and moving forward into an immediate future. The second time element was an element of past time, one which represented these same characters as acting and as being acted upon not only by the events and conflicts of the life around them, but by all the accumulated impact of man's memory and experience so that each moment of his life was conditioned not only by what he saw and felt and did and experienced in that moment, but by all that he had seen and felt and done and experienced and had been in the process of becoming up to that moment. In addition to these two time elements, there was a third which I conceived as being not only time past and present, but as time immutable, as time fixed, unchanging, subject neither to past or present time, as, for instance, the time of rivers, mountains, oceans, and the earth; as time everlasting, a kind of eternal and unchanging world and universe of time against which would be projected the transience of man's life, the bitter briefness of his day. It was this problem, the tremendous, and almost unsolvable problem of these three time elements that almost defeated me and that cost me countless hours of anguish and frustration in the years that were to follow.

As the extent, complexity, and staggering labor of my problem began to dawn upon me, as I began to realize the true nature of the task I had set for myself, what I was up against, the image of the river to which I have referred several times began to haunt my mind. I actually felt that I had a great river pent up and thrusting for release inside of me and that the thing that it was searching for, the thing I had to find for it was a channel into which and through which its flood-like power could pour. I think I can describe the labor for the next two years as being the constant, desperate, and unending search to find a channel for that river. I knew I had to find it or I would be whelmed under by my own flood, drowned in my own secretions, destroyed in the pent up flood of my own creation, and I am sure that every artist who ever lived and wrought as I did has had the same experience.

Meanwhile, while I sought for this release, this channel that I had to find, I was being baffled and haunted everywhere by the nature of a fixed and impossible idea whose error at the time I did not fully apprehend. I was convinced at that time that this whole gigantic plan had to be realized within the limits of a single book which would be called *The October Fair.* I was convinced that somehow I must get into the pages of a single book, embody in every word and phrase and sentence and in every page that I should write the dense and multiple interweavings of this whole gigantic time scheme, this triple web of present, past, and everlasting time in which the substance was all included. And the real reason for this error, the reason for all the failure and confusion which would attend my efforts for the next year or two as I sought to find the channel for my river was simply this: I did not even yet understand the full extent of my material, the nature of the task which I had set myself, to know that I could never get it all within the limits of a single book. My plan was good; in its fundamental conception it had changed little. My error lay in the fact that although I understood my plan, I did not understand its true extent; I had not yet defined its utter limits. As a result I had bitten off more than I could chew.

I kept struggling with the hopeless problem of getting all my material and the dense web of three great elements of time within the pages of one book. It was not until more than a year had passed, when I realized finally that what I had to deal with was material which covered almost 150 years in history, demanded the action of more than two thousand characters, and would in its final design include almost every racial type and social class of American life, that I realized that even the pages of a book of two hundred thousand words were wholly inadequate for the purpose.

How did I finally arrive at this conclusion? I think it is not too much to say that I simply wrote myself into it. I finally understood the nature and extent of my task through my own sweat and labor. It took me another year, a year, that is, after my return from Europe in the spring of 1931, to get there, and I think that it was only then, almost three years after the publication of my first book, that I really saw light, that I really began with some clear, definite, and coherent idea to construct the series of books, to understand the logical divisions of my material, the structural form and sequence which each would take. During all that year, I was writing furiously, almost frantically, feeling now for the first time the full pressure and threat of inexorable time, the necessity for reaching some finality, the necessity to finish something. And now, indeed, during this year the narrative, incident, and character of the books did begin to come. I wrote like mad; I finished scene after scene, chapter after chapter. The characters began to come to life, to grow and multiply until they were numbered by the hundreds, but so huge was the extent of my design, as I now desperately realized, that I can liken these chapters, scenes, and incidents only to a row of sparks and lonely looking lights which one sometimes sees at night from the windows of a speeding train, strung out across a dark and lonely countryside.

I would work furiously day after day and week after week until my mind was stumbling with fatigue, my creative energies utterly exhausted, and although at the end of such a period I would have completed another section and written perhaps as much as two hundred thousand words, enough in itself to make a very long book, I would realize with a feeling of horrible apprehension and despair that what I had completed was only one small section of a single book.

During this time I reached that state of utter, naked need, utter, lonely isolation which every artist has got to reach, meet, live through somehow, and conquer if he is to survive at all. Before this I had been sustained by my own hopeful optimism, by the kindly encouragement and good faith of friends, by that delightful and happy illusion of power and success which we all have when we dream about the books we are going to write, the great works we are going to accomplish, instead of actually doing them. Now I was up against it, face to face with it, and suddenly I realized that there was no escape from it, no getting away from this thing, that I had committed my life, my honor, and my integrity so irrevocably to this struggle that I must conquer now or be destroyed. I was alone with my own work, and suddenly I realized that I had to be alone with it, that no one could come near me now or help me with it no matter how anyone might wish to help. It was like being alone in a lonely place with a desperate, determined antagonist and to know that one can look nowhere for help save in himself, that there is no help save in himself, in his own spirit and in the might and power of his two hands, and that he must meet his foe and conquer him or die himself. For the first time I realized another terrible and naked fact which every artist must finally meet and know, and that is that in a man's work, the thing he lives to do and without which he has nothing, there are contained not only the seeds of life, but the seeds of death, and that that thing which gives us life, that power of work and creation which we have in us and which sustains us and enriches us, will also destroy us like a leprosy if we let it rot stillborn in our vitals. I had to get it out of me somehow. I saw that now. I was too far committed, my life was too far gone with it, there was no escape and no retreat. And now for the first time a poisonous and terrible doubt began to creep into my mind that I might not live long enough to get it out of me, that I had created a labor so large and so impossible that the energy and duration of a dozen lifetimes would not suffice for its accomplishment.

During this time, however, I was sustained by one piece of inestimable good fortune. It was my good fortune to have for a friend a man who is, I believe, not only the greatest editor of his time, but a man whose character is also a character of immense and patient wisdom and a gentle but unyielding fortitude. I think that I may say the chief reason I was not destroyed at this time by the sense of hopelessness and defeat which these gigantic and apparently fruitless labors had awakened in me was largely because of the courage and patience of this man. I did not give in because he would not let me give in, and I think it is also true that at this particular time he had the advantage of being in the position of a skilled and highly experienced observer of a battle. I was, myself, engaged in that battle, covered by its dust and sweat and exhausted by its struggle, and I think it is certain that at this time I understood far less clearly than my friend the nature and the progress of the struggle in which I was engaged. At this time there was little that this man could do except observe, and in one way or another keep me at my task, and in one way or another, in many quiet and marvelous ways he succeeded in doing this.

There is little else that he could do at just this time because I was now at the place where no one could help me very much except myself. I was now at the place where I must produce, and even the greatest editor of his time can do little for a writer until he has produced, until he has brought from the secret darkness, the locked door of his own self into the common light of day the completed concrete accomplishment of his soul's imagining. My friend, the editor, has likened his own function at this trying time to that of a man who is trying to hang on to the fin of a plunging whale, but hang on he did, and it is to his tenacity that I owe my final accomplishment. He did many other things during this time whose beneficent effect upon my spirit was incalculable. For example, almost three years had gone by not only since the publication of my first book, but since anything at all of mine had appeared in print. Meanwhile little whispers, rumors, gossips had begun to spring up, which had perhaps only trivial annoyance to a man sure of his purpose and certain of his final accomplishment, but which can become almost maddening to a man struggling for his life, as it seems to him, and still groping blindly and desperately to find a way out. People were beginning to ask more insistently than ever when my next book would be ready, and now I would sometimes notice a note of scepticism in their question, a kind of doubting inquiry in their eyes. Sometimes people who had read my book would write me letters, ask where the next one was, want to know what the trouble was, what had happened to me that I had not produced another one, and some would even ask if I had written all I had to write, said in one first book all that I had to say. Some of the critics had spoken well of my first book but had also voiced politely sceptical questions which are often asked about first books, particularly first books like mine which are supposed to be directly autobiographical: could the author produce anything else or was he finished with his first attempt?

One morning I opened the paper to read in the daily column of a well-known reviewer a discussion of certain young writers who had started well but who had apparently lost what the critic called the will to write, and it was maddening and absurd, for what it seemed to me that I had lost was not the will to write, but the will to stop from writing. There was nothing I could do, nothing I could say. I had no means to prove myself or answer the accusation, and the sight of those works was like pouring venom in a raw wound.

Meanwhile, however, during the autumn and winter of that grim year, my creative power was functioning at the highest intensity it had ever known. Shortly after the beginning of the year, I finished a large section of the book, later to be published separately as *The Portrait of Bascom Hawke*, and early in the spring I finished another, the story of a woman's life told in her own words. This, I realized, even before I had finished it, was outside the design and temper of the book, but I completed it and in the spring of 1932 these two stories, *The Portrait of Bascom Hawke* and *The Web of Earth*, each of them over thirty thousand words long, were printed in separate issues of *Scribner's Magazine* as short novels. The restorative power that the publication of these two pieces had upon my confidence was immense, and the whole thing was directly due to the wisdom, sagacity, and intuition of the great editor whom I have mentioned.

This was not the only benefit. Although I was unaware of the fact at the time, *Scribner's Magazine* was conducting a contest for the best short novel. *The Portrait of Bascom Hawke* was entered into this contest by the editors of the magazine, and I was fortunate enough to win it, or rather, to share the prize for first place with another manuscript. As a result of this unexpected good fortune, my confidence in my abilities was not only bolstered up, but I was enabled to live for another year on my share of the prize money. I worked hard and steadily through the summer, autumn, and through the winter of 1933. The completed manuscript had already grown to staggering proportions, and my creative powers reached, I believe, the most fertile and prolific quality of performance that they had ever known. But I was beginning to grow very tired after almost three years of steady writing, and my efforts to assimilate into a single volume material which had already reached a length of approximately two million words. I now began to see plainly that from this material the manuscript of at least two long books had begun to take shape, and that it would be absolutely impossible and also wrong to attempt an unnatural compression of two entirely different books into a single novel.

The spring of 1933 found me very tired, but in the spring of that year, out of my new production *Scribner's Magazine* accepted three more long pieces which were published in the spring and summer of that year as long stories. Their names and the order of their publication were: "Death the Proud Brother," which, I think, contained the best writing I had done up to that time, "The Train and the City," and "No

Door." The publication of these pieces also helped to revive my confidence, to earn a little money, which I needed badly, and, perhaps, to keep my name from being utterly forgotten by the public. But that year, I think, was the worst year I have ever known. Before the year was over I was a creature stumbling with fatigue, almost bereft of hope, almost ready to admit defeat, to admit that I was done for as writer, and could not possibly complete the work I had set out to do. It was a black time.

I wrote at times without hope, without belief that I would ever finish, with nothing in me but black despair, and yet I wrote and wrote and could not give up writing. And it seemed that despair itself was the very spurring goad that urged me on, that made me write even when I had no belief that I would ever finish. It seemed to me that my life in Brooklyn, although I had been there only two and a half years, went back through centuries of time, through ocean depths of black and bottomless experience which no ordinary scale of hours or days or weeks or months would ever measure. People have sometimes asked me what happened to my life during these years. They have asked me how I ever found time to observe or see or feel or gather new experience or know anything that was going on in the world of men about me when my life was so completely absorbed by this world of writing and creation. Well, it may seem to be an extraordinary and contradictory fact, but the truth is that never in a similar period of time in my whole life have I been as intensely aware, have I lived so passionately, vividly, and fully, have I shared so richly and with such genuine sympathy and understanding in the common life of man as I did during these years of terrific labor when I was struggling with the giant problem of my own work.

I think the reason for this is less contradictory, much simpler than it seems on first reflection. For one thing, my whole sensory and creative equipment, my powers of feeling and reflection, sense of observation — even the sense of hearing, and above all, my powers of memory — had reached the greatest degree of sharpness and alertness that they had ever known. At the end of the day of savage, grinding labor, my mind was still blazing with its effort, could in no way or by no opiate of reading, poetry, music, alcohol, or any pleasure be appeased or put at rest. I was unable to sleep, unable to subdue or control the raging tumult of these creative energies, and as a result of this condition, for three years I prowled the streets, explored the huge jungle, the swarming web of the million-footed city and came to know it and all its thousand aspects as I had never known it before. I found out more about the city and about America in those three years, I was drawn closer to the life of average man, I became more familiar with his ways, his speech, his thought, his character, and all the million shabby, groping, sordid, mistaken, and somehow valiant aims and aspirations of his million lives than I had ever done before. It was a black time in the history of the nation, a black time in my own life and spirit, and, I suppose, it is but natural that my own picture of that time, my own memory of it now should be a pretty grim and painful one.

Everywhere around me, during these years, I saw the evidence of an incalculable ruin and suffering. My own people, the members of my own family, had been ruined, had lost all the material wealth and accumulation of a lifetime in what was called the "depression." And that universal calamity had somehow struck the life of almost every one I knew. Moreover, in this endless quest and prowling of the night through the great web and jungle of the city, I saw, lived, felt, and experienced the full weight of that horrible human calamity.

I saw a man whose life had subsided into a mass of shapeless and filthy rags, devoured by vermin; wretches huddled together for a little warmth in freezing cold squatting in doorless closets upon the foul seat of a public latrine within the very shadow, the cold shelter of palatial and stupendous monuments of wealth. I saw acts of sickening violence and cruelty, the menace of brute privilege, a cruel and corrupt authority trampling ruthlessly below its feet the lives of the poor, the weak, the wretched, and defenseless of the earth.

And the huge sum, the staggering impact of this black picture of man's inhumanity to his fellow man, the horrible and unending repercussions of these scenes of suffering, violence, oppression, hunger, cold, and filth and poverty going on unheeded, unnoticed, cruelly and indifferently ignored in a world in which the rich and privileged were still rotten with their wealth left a scar upon my life, a conviction in my soul which I shall never lose. It was a black, a bitter, and a brutal time, and, I suppose that this huge chronicle of injustice, ugliness and suffering, gained an added darkness, a heightened anguish from the anguish and frustration of my own spirit at that time, but it is also true that I have never lived so intensely and so richly or shared with such a passionate and sympathetic understanding in man's common life as I did during those three years. That blind, kaleidoscope of night, that century of tormented living when I strove with my own demons and wrought upon the making of a book.

And from it all, curiously and marvelously, there has come as the final deposit, the soul, the essence of all that period of defeat and torment and black suffering, a glorious memory, a certain evidence of the fortitude of man, his ability to suffer and endure, not to complain, and somehow to survive. And it is for this reason now that I think I shall always remember this black period with a kind of joy, with a pride and faith and deep affection that I could not at that time have believed possible, for it was during this time that I somehow survived defeat and lived my life through to a first completion, and through the struggle, suffering, and labor of my own life came to share those qualities in the lives of people all around me. And that is another thing which the making of a book has done for me. It has given my life that kind of enlargement and growth which I think the labor and fulfillment of each work does give the artist's life, and insofar as I have known and experienced these things, I think that they have added to my stature.

Late autumn, the early winter of 1933 arrived and with it, it seemed to me, the final doom of an utter, inevitable, and abysmal failure. I still wrote and wrote, but blindly, hopelessly, unknowingly, like a machine that can't be stopped, that won't run down, and like an old horse, blind with its years of labor and fatigue who endlessly turns the wheel and trots around in a blind, unending circle of a treadmill and knows no other end nor purpose for his life than this. If I slept at night, it was to sleep a sleep that was no sleep, that had no elements of rest or curative oblivion in it, a sleep that was just an unending nightmare of pageantry, of blazing visions that swept all through the night across the fevered and unresting mind of the sleeper, a sleeper who lay there on his bed a witness and spectator of his own visions, who lay there knowing that he slept, was conscious at each moment that he dreamed and that he could at any moment that he wished to wake. And when I woke, it was now to wake exhausted, weary of my life, not knowing where to turn or what to do, not knowing anything but work, and knowing only work itself without a hope, a blind necessity to work without belief, and so stumbling into work again, goading and lashing myself on into a hopeless labor, and so furiously at it through the day; and then night again, exhausted, a tormented and unresting man, a frenzied prowling of a thousand streets, the rusty, manswarm jungle of the earth that bears the name of Brooklyn, and so to bed and sleepless sleep again, the nightmare pageantry, demented visions to which my consciousness lay chained a spectator.

There was a kind of dream which I can only summarize as dreams of Guilt and Time. Chameleon-like in all their damnable and unending fecundities, they restored to me the whole huge world that I had known, the billion faces and the million tongues, and they restored it to me with the malevolent triumph of a passive and unwanted ease. My daily conflict with Amount and Number, the huge accumulations of my years of struggle with the forms of life, my brutal and unending efforts to record upon my memory each brick and paving stone of every street that I had ever walked upon, each face of every thronging crowd in every city, every country with which my spirit had contested its savage and uneven struggle for supremacy—they all returned now—each stone, each street, each town, each country—yes, even every book in the library whose loaded shelves I had tried vainly to devour at college—they returned upon the wings of these mighty, sad, and somehow quietly demented dreams—I saw and heard and knew them all at once, was instantly without pain or anguish, with the calm consciousness of God, master of the whole universe of life against whose elements I had contended vainly for all-knowledge for so many years. And the fruit of that enormous triumph, the calm and instant passivity of that inhuman and demented immortality, was somehow sadder and more bitter than the most galling bitterness of defeat in my contention with the multitudes of life had ever been.

For above that universe of dreams there shone forever a tranquil, muted, and unchanging light of time. And through the traffic of those thronging crowds—whose faces, whose whole united and divided life was now instantly and without an effort of the will, my *own*—there rose forever the sad unceasing murmurs of the body of this life, the vast recessive fadings of the shadow of man's death that breathes forever with its dirge-like sigh around the huge shores of the world.

And *beyond, beyond*—forever *above, around, behind* the vast and tranquil consciousness of my spirit that now held the earth and all her elements in the huge clasp of its effortless subjection—there dwelt forever the fatal knowledge of my own inexpiable *guilt*.

I did not know what I had done—I only knew that I had ruinously forgotten time, and by so doing had betrayed my brother men. I had been long from home—why, how, or in what way, I could not know—but drugged there in the drowsy fumes of some green country of the witches' magic, with something in me dark and full of grief I could not quite remember. And suddenly I was home again—walking alone beneath that light of tranquil, quiet, and unchanging brown, walking the roads, the hill-slopes, and the streets of my familiar country—sometimes the *exact* and *actual* lineaments of home, my childhood, and my native town, so that not only all that I had known and remembered—each familiar street and face and house and every cobblestone upon the pavement—but countless things I never knew that I had seen, or had forgotten that I ever knew—a rusty hinge upon the cellar door, the way a stair creaked, or an old cracked blister of brown paint upon the woodwork by the grate, an oak tree trunk upon the hill all hollowed out upon one side by a knotted hole, the glazed pattern of the glass in the front door, the brass handle of a street-car brake-control, quite rubbed to silver on one side by the hard grip of the motorman, and covered by a cloth tobacco sack—such things as these, together with a million others, returned now to torment my sleep.

And even more than these, more, more familiar even than these scenes of memory and inheritance, were those landscapes that somehow had been *derived* from them—the streets, the towns, the houses and the faces that I saw and imagined not the way they *were*, but the way they *should* be in the unfathomed, strange, and unsuspected logics of man's brain and heart—and that were, on this account, more real than realness, and more true than home.

I had been long from home—I had grown old in some evil and enchanted place, I had allowed my life to waste and rot in the slothful and degrading surfeits of Circean time. And now my life was lost—my work undone—I had betrayed my home, my friends, my people in the duties of some solemn and inviolable trust—and suddenly I was home again, and *silence* was my answer!

They did not look at me with looks of bitterness and hate, they did not lash me with the fierce opprobrium of scorn, or curse me with the menaces of vengeance and reprisal—oh, if they had, what balm of anguish and of judgment even curses would have had!—but instead their look was silence, and their tongue was mute. And again, again, I walked the streets of that familiar town, and after years of absence saw again the features of familiar faces, and heard familiar words, the sounds of well-known voices once again, and with a still and deep amazement saw the shift and interplay of action, the common familiarity of day, the traffic of the streets, and saw that it was all as it had always been, I had forgotten nothing—until I passed them, and death fell.

I walked among them, and their movements ceased, I walked among them, and their tongues were still, I walked among them and they neither moved nor spoke until I passed, and if they looked at me, their eyes were blank with silence and no memory; there was no reproach, no grief, and no contempt, there was no bitterness and scorn — if I had died, there should at least have been the ghost of memory, but it was as if I never had been born. And so I passed them by, and everywhere I trod was death, and when I had gone by, behind me I could hear their voices start again; the clamors of the street, and all the traffic of bright day awoke — but only after I had passed them by!

And so the whole town flowed around me, was behind me, and at once, without a bridge or instant of transition, I was walking on a barren road, across the huge sweep of a treeless waste and barren vacancy and that tranquil, sad and fatal light shone on me from the horror of a planetary vacancy, the lidless and remorseless eye of an unperturbed sky that ate into my naked spirit constantly the acid of unuttered shame.

Another and more pertinent variety of these dreams of Guilt and Time would take this form: It seemed to me that I had gone abroad, was living there, and yet was conscious that I was still employed as an instructor at the university. Remote from all the violence and turmoil of America, the harsh impact of its daily life, remote too from the rasping jargon of the university, its corridors packed with swarthy faces, loud with strident tongues, away from all the jar and rush and hurly-burly of its fevered life, its unwholesome tensions and its straining nerves, I lived my life in foreign luxuries of green and gold. I dreamed my life away in ancient Gothic towns, or in the pleasant romance of a château country, my spirit slid from land to land, from one enchantment to another, my life .

was passing by in spells of drowsy magic—and yet I was forever haunted by a consciousness of Time and Guilt, the obscure gnawing of forsaken trust. And suddenly I would seem to wake into a full and frenzied consciousness: I had been gone from home a year—my classes at the university had been waiting on me—and instantly I was there again, rushing through those swarming corridors, hurrying frantically from one classroom to another, trying desperately to find the classes I had so forgotten. There was a grotesque and horrible quality of humor in these dreams, which unfortunately I could not appreciate: I was somehow convinced my forlorn classes had been seeking for me for a year, I saw them searching through the mazes of the corridors, prowling among the swarming myriads of their thirty thousand fellow students, sitting in patient dejection at the hours appointed for our meetings in classrooms where their absent teacher never entered. And finally—and most horrible of all—I saw the mounting pile of unmarked student themes—those accursed themes that grew in number week by week—that piled up in mountainous and hopeless accumulations—whose white backs were hideously innocent of the scrawled comment with which I had once—tormented by twin agonies of boredom and conscience—covered every scrap of their surface. And now it was too late! Even a month, two weeks, a week—some miracle of time and frenzied labor—might have served somehow to retrieve myself—but now it was the last day of the term, the last class ended, the last irrevocable moment of salvation had gone by. I found myself suddenly standing there in the offices of the English faculty, struck dumb with horror, confronted by the great white mountain of those unmarked themes. I turned, a ring of silent forms encircled me, not staring, not harsh with scorn or anger, and not thrusting close, but just looking at me with the still surveyal of their condemnation. My little Jews stood first, their dark eyes fixed on me with a dejected but unwavering reproach, and behind them stood the jury of my peers, the outer circle of instructors.

They were all there — students, instructors, friends, enemies, and the huge damnation of that pile of unmarked themes — there was no word spoken, nothing but their quiet look of inflexible and unpardoning accusal.

This dream returned to torture sleep a hundred times: Each time I would awake from it in a cold sweat of anguish and of horror, and so strong was the impression of the dream, so real and terrible the spell of its conviction, that sometimes I would wake out of this dream and lie for minutes in cold terror while my mind fought with the phantoms of my sleep to argue me back into reality.

Nor were these dreams of Guilt and Time the only ones: my mind and memory in sleep blazed with a fiery river of unending images: the whole vast reservoirs of memory were exhumed and poured into the torrents of this fiery flood, a million things, once seen and long forgotten, were restored and blazed across my vision in this stream of light — and a million million things unseen, the faces, cities, streets, and landscapes yet unseen and long imagined — the unknown faces yet more real than these that I had known, the unheard voices more familiar than the voices I had heard forever, the unseen patterns, masses, shapes and landscapes in their essence far more real than any actual or substantial fact that I had ever known — all streamed across my fevered and unresting mind the flood of their unending pageantry — and suddenly I knew that it would never end.

For sleep was dead forever, the merciful, dark and sweet oblivions of childhood sleep. The worm had entered at my heart, the worm lay coiled and feeding at my brain, my spirit, and my memory—I knew that finally I had been caught in my own fire, consumed by my own hungers, impaled on the hook of that furious and insatiate desire that had absorbed my life for years. I knew, in short, that one bright cell in the brain or heart or memory would now blaze on forever—by night, by day, through every waking, sleeping moment of my life, the worm would feed and the light be lit,—that no anodyne of food or drink, or friendship, travel, sport or woman could ever quench it, and that nevermore until death put its total and conclusive darkness on my life, could I escape.

I knew at last I had become a writer: I knew at last what happens to a man who makes the writer's life his own.

Such was the state my life had come to in the early winter of 1933, and even at that moment, although I could not see it, although I was past seeing it, although I could no longer believe or hope for such impossible good fortune, the end of my great labor was in sight. In the middle of December of that year the great editor, of whom I have spoken, and who, during all this tormented period of struggle and frustration, had kept a quiet but vigilant watch upon me, called me to his home and quietly informed me that my book was finished. I could not believe him. I could not credit my own hearing. I could only look at him with stunned surprise, and finally I could only tell him out of that bottomless depth of my own hopelessness, that he was mistaken, that the book was not finished, that it could never be completed, that I was unequal to the task, that I could write no more. He answered with the same quiet finality that the book was finished whether I knew it or not, and he told me then to go to my room and spend the next week in collecting in its proper order the manuscript which had accumulated during the last two years.

I followed his instructions, still without hope and without belief. I worked for six days sitting in the middle of the floor surrounded by mountainous stacks of typed manuscript on every side. At the end of a week I had the first part of it together, and just two days before Christmas, 1933, I delivered to him the manuscript of *The October Fair*, and a few days later, the manuscript of *The Hills Beyond Pentland*. The manuscript of *The Fair* was, at that time, something over one million words in length. He had seen most of it in its dismembered fragments as I had brought them in to him during the three preceding years, but now, for the first time, he was seeing it in its sequential order, and once again his marvelous intuition was right; he had told me the truth when he said that I had finished the book.

It was not finished in its final and completed form; it was not even finished at that time in any way that was publishable or readable. It was really not a book so much as it was the skeleton of a book, but for the first time in four years the skeleton was all there. It was at last assembled. The continuity of the book, all of the main elements from beginning to end, were coherently, concretely, and indisputably there. An enormous labor of revision, weaving together, shaping, molding, ordering, and, above all, cutting remained, but I had the book now so that nothing, not even the despair and hopelessness of my own spirit, could take it from me. He told me so, and suddenly I saw that he was right.

From that moment my spirit was on the mend. It was like being born again. I was like a man who has been utterly, irrevocably lost, and who suddenly, in a way he never dared to dream or hope, has found himself again: like a man who is drowning and who suddenly, at the last gasp of his final dying effort, feels earth beneath his feet again. My spirit was overwhelmed by a sensation of the greatest joy and triumph it had ever known, and although my mind was tired, my body exhausted, from that moment on I felt equal to anything on earth.

It took the editor about two weeks of unceasing labor to read and estimate the enormous manuscript. At the end of that time, we were ready to begin our work—perhaps I could better say our collaboration, although that term, I know, would embarass him.

It was evident that a tremendous amount of work and many difficult and serious problems were before us, but now "we" had the thing. For the first time he had something we could work together on, and we welcomed the labor before us with happy confidence. What was the nature of some of the problems which we had to meet and face before the book, or at least the first of these books, could be made ready for the press? In the first place there was the problem of the book's gigantic length. Even in this skeletonized form the manuscript of *The October Fair* was over a million words in length, which is about twelve times the length of the average novel or twice the length of *War and Peace*. It was manifest, therefore, that it would not only be utterly impossible to publish such a manuscript in a single volume, but that even if it were published in several volumes, a proceeding which was unheard of with a young writer who has published only one book, the tremendous length of such a manuscript would practically annihilate its chances of ever finding a public which would read it.

It now became evident, also, that long as this manuscript was, it was, in itself, only a part of a much longer work, and that, together with the manuscript of *The Hills Beyond Pentland*, it formed two in a series of books of which the total number would be five or six. This presented another problem which was very serious from an editorial and publishing point of view. If these various books were published separately and brought out in the proper sequence of their appearance, would each of them be whole and unified enough to satisfy a reader's desire for finality—that is for a beginning, a middle, and an end—or would they seem to end inconclusively, in other words, to be only enormous fragments of an even more enormous whole? This was a very grave problem, a very serious difficulty because it affected not only the life of one book, the favorable response that we both hoped, of course, it might have, but it affected vitally the continuing life of all the books that were to follow. In other words, we not only wanted to do all we could to assure the favorable reception of the first book to be published, but we hoped also through that book to sustain and increase the public interest in the whole design for all of the books which were to follow.

This problem now faced us, and the editor grappled with it immediately. For some time, a week or two, we debated the matter, and at one time he was, himself, so baffled with the staggering size of the manuscript which constituted, he said, a problem that was unique not only in his own publishing experience, but also, he thought, in the entire annals of American publishing. He was so baffled with this problem for a time that he even contemplated meeting it in an extraordinary way that would also have been unique in the annals of American publishing. He was determined, now that he had the manuscript at last, that it would get published somehow no matter what its length might be, and he was ready if need be, he told me, to publish even if he had to break all the rules and precedents of publishing in order to do it.

Thus, for a short time, the editor contemplated bringing out the book in sections, publishing the manuscript in separate volumes, perhaps two hundred thousand words each, regardless of whether any volume reached a definite conclusion, the main object being to publish and publish until the whole work should be complete. It was an unheard of experiment, but the editor found it a fascinating one, and although it had never been tried before, his intuition told him that it might succeed. Fortunately he found another way out.

As his examination of the manuscript of *The October Fair* proceeded, he found that the book did describe two complete and separate cycles. The first of these cycles was a movement which described the period of unrest, wandering, search, and hunger in a man's youth. The second cycle described the period of greater certitude, of intenser concentration, and was dominated by a unity of a single passion. In the first cycle the scene changed rapidly and constantly from place to place, from city to city, from country to country. This part of the book was a chronicle of trains and cities, oceans, ships, and voyages, departure, wandering and return, the shifting web and interplay of life in many different scenes and places, a chronicle of all the confused desires, the tormented hopes and wanderings of youth. The second cycle had more of the unity of formal design. The scene was, for the most part, the scene of a great city, a great rock of life, and although the swarming life of the great city, the bewildering variety and complexity of its forms were represented, all were coherent with a central unity of a great rock, of flashing tides, bounded round, and the emotions of love and death which govern the central narrative.

It was obvious, therefore, that what we had in the two cyclic movements of this book was really the material of two completely different chronicles, and although the second of the two, the one about the city and its life, was by far the more finished and complete—the pieces published as "Death the Proud Brother" and "No Door" were parts of this—the first cycle, of course, was the one which logically we ought to complete and publish first, and after careful consideration and reflection, we decided on this course.

We took the first part first. I immediately prepared a long and minutely thorough synopsis which described not only the course and action of the book from first to last, but which also included an analysis of those chapters which had been completed in their entirety, of those which were completed only in part, and of those which had not been written at all, and with this synopsis before us, we set to work immediately to prepare the book for press. This work occupied me throughout the whole of the year 1934. The book was completed at the beginning of 1935, and was published in March of that year under the title of *Of Time and the River*.

It may, perhaps, be of some practical interest to some of you if I attempt some description here of the nature of the editor's work upon such a manuscript as mine. The problem, as has been shown, was an extraordinary one. The need for editing and for editorial assistance was very great. There was never a case where an editor was more badly needed and where his services were of more practical value. In the first place, the manuscript, even in its unfinished form, called for the most radical cutting, and because of the nature of my own method, the way in which the book had been written, as well as the fatigue which I now felt, I was not well prepared to do by myself the task that lay ahead of us.

Cutting had always been the most difficult and distasteful part of writing to me; my tendency had always been to write rather than to cut. My critical faculty, although very clear and sharp at times where the work of other writers was concerned, was very uncertain and perplexed where my own work was concerned. One is often told glibly to cut ruthlessly, to cut one's manuscript to the bone, to be relentless in the excision of one's own work. Unfortunately, there is not much point in cutting ruthlessly unless one knows exactly where the ruthlessness should begin and end. One can admire the skill and stern precision of a surgeon, but one does not like to see people make wild and incoherent gestures with a knife. Moreover, whatever critical faculty I may have had concerning my own work had been seriously impaired, for the time being at least, by the frenzied labor of the past four years. During the course of this unremitting struggle, my life had become so involved finally, so completely absorbed by the work I was doing, that it was now almost impossible for me to detach myself from it sufficiently to get any kind of critical perspective whatever. A labor of ruthless excision was now obviously necessary—an excision that would deal not with phrases, words, or paragraphs or an occasional page or two, but which would deal with hundreds of pages, hundreds of thousands of words. When a man's work has poured from him for almost five years like burning lava pouring from a volcano; when all of it, however mistaken, disproportionate and superfluous, has been heated by his life, given fire and passion at a white heat of his own creative energy, has come from him in a flooding, fiery river of creation, it is very difficult suddenly to become coldly surgical, critically impersonal, ruthlessly detached.

To give a few concrete illustrations of the difficulties that now confronted us: The opening section of the book describes the journey of a train across the State of Virginia at night. Its function in the book is simply to introduce some of the chief characters, to indicate a central situation, to give something of the necessary information, the essential background from which the book proceeds, and perhaps through the movement of the train across the stillness of the earth to establish a certain beat, evoke a certain emotion which is proper and inherent to the nature of the book. Such a section, therefore, undoubtedly serves an important and essential function, but in proportion to the whole aim and purport of the book, its function is a secondary and auxiliary one and must, therefore, be related to the whole book in a proportionate way.

Now in the original version, the manuscript which described the journey of the train across Virginia at night, which introduced certain characters and told something about the lives of some of the characters on the train, was well over one hundred thousand words in length, or considerably longer than the longest novel. Now a very interesting novel could be written about a great American train, and perhaps someday I shall try to write one because trains, the life of trains, the people on trains, the sounds that trains make, the effect that a train has upon man's memory, upon his senses and emotions, have always interested me profoundly, but here definitely, at the beginning of a book which should be started swiftly, there was no place for an exhaustive treatise upon trains and the lives and characters of those passengers. Here what was needed was just an introductory chapter or two, and what I had written was over one hundred thousand words long, and I may add that this same difficulty, this lack of proportion, was also evident in other parts of the manuscript.

What I had written about the great train was really good. It came from a whole lifetime of thinking, feeling, and observing trains. But what I now had to face, the very bitter lesson that every one who wants to write has got to learn, was that a thing may in itself be good, excellent, splendid, the finest, truest piece of writing one has ever done, and yet have absolutely no place in the manuscript one hopes to publish.

This is a hard thing, but it must be faced, and so we faced it.

My train did have a place at the beginning of my book, a definite and proper one, but it did not have one hundred thousand words of place. And so we cut it ruthlessly, my editor, the directing force, until we had reduced its bulk to less than thirty thousand words.

My spirit quivered at the bloody execution. My soul recoiled before the carnage of so many lovely things cut out upon which my heart was set, but it had to be done, and we did it. The first chapter in the original manuscript, a chapter which the editor, himself, admitted was as good a single piece of writing as I had ever done, was relentlessly kicked out, and the reason it was kicked out was that it was really not a true beginning for the book but merely something which led up to the true beginning; therefore it had to go.

And so it went all up and down the line. My great fault — a fault of great excessiveness, a general too-muchness — has been conditioned somewhat by the fact that I do not always know when I have said enough. It comes, perhaps, from a certain lack of confidence in my own powers and a certain lack of confidence in the perceptions of my readers so that often, having said a thing, I will go back and say it over in another way in the hope that somehow I will make it plain, that by excess I will get it understood. This fault we had to grapple with all through the book. The editor performed miracles in cutting. Chapters fifty thousand words long were reduced to ten or fifteen thousand words, and having faced this inevitable necessity, I finally acquired a kind of ruthlessness of my own, and once or twice, myself, did more cutting than he was willing to allow.

Another fault that has always troubled me in writing is that I have often attempted to reproduce in its entirety the full flood and fabric of a scene in life itself. Thus, in another section of the book, four people were represented as talking to each other for four hours without a break or intermission. All were good talkers; often all talked, or tried to talk, at the same time. The talk was wonderful and living talk because I knew the life and character and the vocabulary of all these people from its living source, and I had forgotten nothing. Yet all the time, all that was actually happening in this scene was that a young woman had got out of her husband's motor car and gone into her mother's house and kept calling to the impatient man outside every time he honked his horn, "All right. All right. I'll be with you in five minutes." These five minutes really lengthened into four hours, while the unfortunate man outside honked upon his horn, and while the two women and two young men of the same family inside carried on a torrential discourse and discussed exhaustively the lives and histories of almost everyone in town, their memories of the past, adventures of the present, and speculations of the future. I put it all down in the original manuscript just as I had seen and known and lived it a thousand times, and even if I do say so myself, the nature of the talk, the living vitality and character of the language, the utter naturalness, the floodtide river of it all was wonderful, but I had made four people talk eighty thousand words—two hundred printed pages of close type in a minor scene of an enormous book, and of course, good as it was, it was all wrong and had to go.

Such, then, were some of our major difficulties with the manuscript we had in hand, and although since its publication there have been many criticisms of its excessive length, many critical declarations to the effect that the book could have achieved its purpose in a shorter compass and would have benefited by a much more radical cutting, the cutting we did do was much more drastic and far-reaching than I had dreamed was possible.

Meanwhile I was proceeding day by day at full speed with the work of completing my design, finishing the unfinished parts and filling in the gaps and the transition links which were essential. This in itself was an enormous job and kept me writing all day long as hard as I could go for a full year. Here again the nature of my chief fault was manifest. I wrote too much again. I not only wrote what was essential, but time and time again my enthusiasm for a good scene, one of those enchanting vistas which can open up so magically to a man in the full flow of his creation would overpower me with its seductive charms, and I would write thousands of words upon a scene which, although in itself good, contributed nothing of vital importance to a book whose greatest need already was ruthless condensation.

During the course of this year, I must have written well over a half million words of additional manuscript, of which, of course, only a small part was finally used.

The nature of my method, the desire fully to explore and investigate my material, to make the fullest and most complete use of it, had led me into another error. I hated to lose any of it. I was unwilling to see any of it go. The whole cumulative effect of those five years of incessant writing had been to make me feel not only that everything had to be used, but that everything had to be told, that nothing could be implied. Therefore, at the end, there were at least a dozen additional scenes and chapters in the book which I felt had to be completed to give the book its final value. I debated this question desperately with my editor a thousand times. I told him that these scenes and chapters had to go in simply because I felt the book would not be complete without them, and with every persuasive and reasonable argument he had, he tried to show me that I was wrong in this, that the effect I hoped to achieve had already been achieved without these chapters, that it would therefore be a mistake to include them. I see now that on the whole he was right about it, but at the time I was so exhausted with my work, so close to it, so inextricably involved, that I did not have the detachment necessary for a true appraisal.

The end came suddenly—the end of those five years of torment, struggle, and incessant productivity. In October I took a trip to Chicago, a two weeks' vacation, my first in over a year. When I returned I found that my editor had quietly and decisively sent the manuscript to the press, the printers were already at work on it, the proof was beginning to come in. I had not foreseen it; I was desperate, bewildered. "You can't do it," I told him, "the book is not yet finished. I must have six months more on it."

To this he answered that the book was not only finished, but that if I took six months more on it, I would then demand another six months and six months more beyond that, and that if I continued, I might very well become so obsessed with this one work that I would never get it published. He went on to say, and I think with complete justice, that such a course was wrong for me, and for the nature of my talent. I was not, he said, a Flaubert kind of writer. I was not a perfectionist. I had twenty, thirty, almost any number of books in me, and the important thing was to get them produced and not to spend the rest of my life in perfecting one book. He agreed that with six months' additional work upon the book, I might improve it somewhat, achieve a certain additional finish and completion, but he did not think that the benefit would be nearly as great, the improvement as extensive, as I thought they would be, and his own deep conviction as my friend and publisher was that the book should be published at once without further delay, that I should get it out of me, forget about it, turn my life and energy to the final completion of the work which was already prepared and ready, waiting for me. He told me, furthermore, exactly what the nature of the criticism would be, the criticism of its length, its adjectives, its over-abundance, but he told me not to despair. He assured me that as a result of those grueling five years of bitter labor, error, groping, and experiment, I had learned a great deal about my profession, a great deal which in my present state of fatigue and nearness to the work just ended was not yet apparent, but that it would become increasingly more apparent as time went on, and in this, too, I believe he was right.

He told me finally that I would go on and do better work, that I would learn to work without so much confusion, waste, and useless torment, that my future books would more and more achieve the unity, sureness, and finality that every artist wants his work to have, but that I had to learn in the way I had learned, searching, groping, struggling, finding my own way for myself, that this was the only way to learn.

What remained after this was just the final work of correcting proofs, organizing, making minor changes and revisions, getting the book ready in its final printed form. Because of its immense size in its final printed version — it was over nine hundred pages long and almost a half million words — there was a great deal of this kind of work. And from that time on I really knew the main job was over. It had been taken from me; it had now undergone the fatal and irrevocable finality of print. For good or ill there was little I could do about it.

In January, 1935, I finished the last of my revisions on the proof; the first printed copies came from the press in February.

The book was released for final publication early in March. I was not here when it came out. I had taken a ship for Europe the week before, and although my spirits had revived temporarily under the excitement and anticipation of the voyage and of departure, the farewells and encouragement of my friends, as the ship got farther and farther from the American shores, my spirits sank lower and lower, reaching, I think, the lowest state of hopeless depression they had ever known. This, I believe, was largely a physical reaction, the inevitable effect of relaxation and idleness upon a human organism which had for five years been strained to its utmost limit. My life at this period really seemed to me to be like a great spring which had been tense and taut for years and which was now slowly uncoiling from it tension. I had the most extraordinary sense of loneliness and empty, naked desolation I had ever known when I thought about my book. I had never realized until now how close I had been to it, how much a part of me it had become, and now that it had been taken away from me, my life felt utterly futile, empty, hollow as a shell. I did not know what to do with myself, where to turn. It was as if some well-loved brother with whom one's whole life has been spent inseparably had died.

And now that the book was gone, now that there was nothing more that I could do about it, I felt the most abysmal sensation of ruin and failure. I have always been somewhat afraid of print, although print is a thing I have tried so hard to achieve—without which what I do is incomplete. Yet it is literally true that with everything I have ever written or had printed, not only my two books, but also all the long and short stories that *Scribner's* and other magazines have published, I have felt at the last moment when the hour of naked print drew nigh a kind of desperation and have even entreated my publisher not only to defer the publication of my book until another season, but have asked the editors of magazines to put off the publication of a story for another month or two until I had a chance to look at it again, work on it some more, do something to it, I was not sure what.

Now this feeling had become overwhelming as the ship approached the coasts of Europe and I realized that my book would be released in another day or two. I had a nameless and overwhelming sense of guilt and shame greater than any I have felt before. I felt as if my life and spirit had been stripped naked, that I had shamefully and ruinously exposed myself, and that from this inexpiable disgrace there could never be any escape, for I was now convinced that the book would be a total, hopeless failure, that through it I had exposed myself as a pitiable fool who had no talent and who once and for all had completely vindicated the prophecies of the critics who had felt the first book was just a flash in the pan. I realize now that most of this was just the result of physical and mental exhaustion, but it produced the most extraordinary and ugly hallucination, the most terrible and exaggerated delusions. I could not, for example, bear to look at my own book. I approached it with fear and trembling and a sense of loathing. I was sure that every page would reveal to me some new and shameful indication of my incompetence and lack of talent, and when I did steel myself to read the book, I could only read a few pages at a time. And when I did, the most trivial things would get me in a frenzy. If I came to typographical error, and I confess there were a great many in the first edition not only because of my own fatigue when I read proof, but because of the haste with which so much of the whole book had been prepared. This whole last volume of a half million words had been made ready for the press in less than a year. But when I saw one of these errors, however trivial, it would become so large that it would seem to spring out at me and explode all over the place so that I could read none of the other words upon the page at all, and I was sure that it would seem this way to every reader, that the book, in addition to being of no worth or merit, would also be a horrible botchwork comedy of errors.

It was in this frame of mind that I arrived in Paris on March 8, the day the book was to be published in America. I had come away to forget about it. I had told myself I would not think of it, that I would eat and sleep, restore my energy, revive my interest in the life among new lands and faces, and above all things, I would not think about my book. And yet I thought about it all the time. I could not forget it. I would sit on the terrace of the Café la Regence and watch the marvelous flash and play of life upon the Avenue de l'Opéra and see the people going past and smell all the smells, the strange, mixed, haunting, fusion of the odors of Paris that qualify its life so magically and that give it so much of its unique tone and texture, and it was all lovely, enchanting, magical, intoxicating as it has always been, and it seemed to me that I had always known it, and yet it was stranger than a dream and I would forget nothing. At night I could not sleep. I prowled the streets from night to morning; at least a dozen times in two short weeks I heard the celebration of mass at Sacré Coeur, and then would walk the streets again and come back home to my hotel at ten o'clock and lie upon the bed, and still I could not sleep.

After several days of this, I steeled myself to go to the office of the travel agency where a message might be waiting for me. I found a cablegram there. It was from my publisher, and it said simply: "Magnificent reviews somewhat critical in ways expected, full of greatest praise." I read it the first time with a feeling of almost intolerable joy and happiness, but as I continued to read and re-read it, the old dark doubt and confusion began to creep across my mind again, and by the time night had come I was convinced that this wonderful cable was just a sentence of doom, and that my editor, out of the infinite kindness and compassion of his spirit, had taken this means of breaking the news to me that my book was an utter and colossal failure. And yet I knew him to be the most honest person I have ever known, a man whose whole nature, even in moments of the greatest success, leaned instinctively toward the side of understatement.

Three days passed in which I prowled the streets of Paris like a maddened animal, and of those three days I could later remember almost nothing. At the end of that time I sent a frenzied cablegram to that editor in which I told him I could stand anything better than this state of damnable uncertainty and pleaded with him to give me the plain, blunt truth no matter how bitter it might be. His answer to this cable was such that I could no longer doubt him or the reception which the book had had at home.

I was still in a bad state, a kind of wild and ungovernable excitement that still drove me on, but gradually I began to quiet down and under the calm and homely atmosphere of England and the renewal of pleasant friendship with the many people I have known there, my energies began to restore themselves.

I stayed away four months, and during that time read none of the reviews and had no letters save one or two from my editor and from a few close friends, and when I returned early in July, I felt completely restored, filled to the brim with a resurgence of creative energy and eager to be at work again. I was immensely happy and elated at the letters and the news I found there, tremendously happy to know I had had a success and enormously grateful to the people who had written me as they did and to know they felt as they said they felt about what I had written. It made me want to exert every energy of my life and talent in an effort to fulfill and justify the belief of all these people. It made me want to surpass by far everything I had done before. And with the joy and confidence the whole experience has given me, and what I hope I have learned, I think I may be able to do it.

This completes, as far as I can remember it, the story of the making of a book and what happened to its maker. I know it is too long a story; I know, also, that it must seem to you a story filled with the record of a man's blunders, uncertainties, errors, and ludicrous mistakes, but simply because it is that kind of story, I hope that it may have some value for some of you. I came out here resolved that whatever else I said to you, I was going to try to tell you the truth without pretense or evasion about the way I wrote a book. I have not told you the story because I think my way is the only way to write a book or because I would suggest such a method to any of you. I do not think it is the way to write a book. I would most earnestly hope that none of you will ever write a book in this fashion, but if it is not the way to write a book, it is at least the way in which one man wrote one, and it is just for this reason, because I have tried to tell you the true story of the artist as a worker rather than of the artist as a fine fellow with fine critical, aesthetical notions, that I hope this story may have some value for some of you. It is a story of the artist as a man and as a worker, as a creature full of toil and sweat and labor and imperfection. It is a story, I think, of the artist not as a fine fellow who is not as other men and who lives in a different world from other men, but is a man who is derived out of the common family of earth, who is compacted of his father's common clay, of sweat and blood and dust and agony and who knows all the anguish, error, and frustration that his father or any man alive can know.

The life of the artist at any age or epoch of man's history has not been an easy one. And here in America, it has often seemed to me, it may well be the hardest life that man has ever known. I do not speak to you in terms of spiritual complaint. I am not speaking to you of some frustration in our native life, some barrenness of spirit, some arid Philistinism which contends against the artist's life and which prevents his growth. I do not speak of these things because I do not put the same belief or credence in them that I once did. I do not speak of them because these are things which, if they exist, exist, I feel, not so much because we are Americans as because men everywhere are what they are, will be what they have been; and I know that Philistinism was not discovered yesterday in Boston and that the race which of all peoples has produced the greatest poets has loved poets and their poetry least. But when I speak as I have spoken of the life of the artist here in America, I am speaking again as I have tried to speak all through this talk in the concrete terms of his actual experience, the nature of the physical task before him. It seems to me that that task is one whose physical proportions are vaster and more difficult than any other nation on the earth can know. It is not merely that in the cultures of Europe and of the Orient the American artist can find no antecedent scheme, no structural plan, no body of tradition that can give his own work the validity and truth that it must have. It is not merely that he must make somehow a new tradition for himself, derived from his own life and from the enormous space and energy of American life, the structure of his own design; it is not merely that he is confronted by these problems; it is even more than this, that the labor of a complete and whole articulation, the discovery of an entire universe and of a complete language is the task that lies before him.

And it is to this task that he must consign his life with all the energy, faith and integrity that are in him. If he is a painter, he must learn to paint colors, structures, shapes, and landscapes that are proper to our native and incomparable life. If he is a musician, he must learn the beat, the tone, the quality of the rhythm that is in our life and ours alone. And if he is a writer, he must learn to speak the tongue that no one in this land has spoken yet — the language and the speech that all of us have known in our hearts, have known with our lives, but can no longer be forgotten or denied and that never yet has found an utterance.

Such is the nature of our task. Such is the nature of the struggle that confronts us, to which henceforth our lives must be devoted. Out of the billion forms, the huge and single substance of America, out of the web, the flash, the thrust, the savage violence and the dense complexity of all its swarming, million-footed life; out of the million little things that we have known all our lives but for which we never found a word; out of every flick and dart of evanescent memory; from all the things remembered and forgotten; from the last and deepest adyt of the ancient and swarm-haunted mind of man; from the unique and single substance of this land and life of ours, must we draw the power and energy of our own life, the articulation of our speech, the substance of our art.

For here it seems to me in hard and honest ways like these we may find the tongue, the language, and the conscience that as men and artists we have got to have. Here, too, perhaps, must we who have no more than what we have, who know no more than what we know, who are no more than what we are, find our America. Here, at this present hour and moment of my life, I seek for mine.

Writing and Living

14

About this time, I began to write. I was editor
of the college paper- which, in my day, and under my
direction, always did have at least, a certain
interest) since it was interesting to examine in this
week's edition the ruins and relics of last month's news.
But in addition to this, I wrote some stories and some
poems for the magazine, of which I was also a member of
the editorial staff. The War was going on then; I was too
young to be in service, and I suppose my first attempts
creatively may be traced to the direct and patriotic
inspiration of the War. I remember one, in particular-
a poem, (I believe, my first) which was aimed
directly at the luckless head of Kaiser Bill. The poem
was called defiantly "The Challenge", and I remember
it was written directly in the style, and according to
the meter, of the present Crisis", by James Russell Lowell.
I remember further that it took a high tone from the very
beginning: the poet, it is said, is the prophet and
prophet and the bard- the awakened tongue of all his folk-
and I was all of that. In the name of embattled democracy,
I let the Kaiser have the works, and I remember two lines
in particular that seemed to me to have a very ringing tone-
"Thou hast given us the challenge- pay, now dog, the cost,
and go!" I remember these lines so well because they were
the occasion of an editorial argument at the time: the
more conservative element on the editorial
staff, felt that the words, "thou dog" were too

A page of the typescript for *Writing and Living,* showing revisions by Thomas Wolfe. Reprinted by permission of the Estate of Thomas Wolfe.

I AM GOING TO TALK SHOP TO you, because my own experience has been that if people have anything at all interesting to say it is likely to be concerned with shop, and because anything I can say to you will have to be concerned with shop. I am coming to you from the shop — my own — where I have been at work for many months. I don't think it matters much where your shop is, as long as you can get your work done in it. For seven or eight months past mine has been in New York City, in an old hotel. I suppose there are better shops and better places to have a shop than the place where I have been; but it has served its purpose very well. In the first place, the old hotel has tremendous rooms, high ceilings, loads of floor space to walk back and forth in — something that more smartly appointed new hotels do not always have. In the second place, the old hotel is not, as hotels in New York go, an expensive one. And in the third place, although I frankly do not believe that hotels are a most desirable permanent place of residence, in New York they do have this advantage: one doesn't have to take a lease — and if one is a writer, with income insecure, and the desire occasionally to travel, that is a big advantage.

Now, I am going to tell you something more about my shop, because for me, at any rate, it is important. I have a big room where I work, and another room where I sleep: I'd like to emphasize the fact of space, because I think almost every capitalistic notion I have begins with space. I can do without a lot of things that many people not only would be uncomfortable without, but think essential. My luxury — and by an ironic paradox, in America of all places, where there is so much space, it has really come to be a luxury — is space. I like to have a big place to work in, and if I don't have it I am uncomfortable. I've tried to describe and emphasize all these apparently trifling physical things to you, because they have been so important to me. I am a writer. And no matter what you may have heard about writers, my own experience has been that a writer is first and foremost a working man. This may surprise you. It does surprise most people. For example, it has always surprised my mother, who is an admirable old woman, seventy-eight years old, who has worked all her life, as hard as any person I've ever known, and who is today as alert, vigorous, active as any person of that age you know. But my mother, like so many other people, has never been able to get it into her head that writing is work. When I was home last summer, she said to me: "Now, boy, if you can get paid for doing the kind of thing you do, you're mighty lucky — for all the rest of your people had to *work* for a living!" I keep reminding her that writing is also work — as hard work, I think, as anyone can do — I keep insisting on the fact; and my mother amiably keeps agreeing. But also she keeps forgetting — and in unguarded moments, I often get flashes of what is really going on in what the psychologists call her subconscious. And apparently, it is something like this: writing is a kind of stunt, a kind of trick which some people are born with — like being a sword-swallower or a left-handed baseball pitcher — and if one is fortunate enough to be born with this trick, or gift, he can, without much effort to himself, be paid for it. I don't believe my mother's views upon the subject are at all extraordinary: in fact, I should say they represented, unconsciously at least, the views of a majority of people everywhere. I know my mother would certainly be surprised, and possibly astonished, if I told her that I thought I was a working man—by this, I mean a man who does actual hard physical labor—in very much the same way as my father was, who was a stone-cutter; and if I told her that I looked upon the big room in which I work—with its crates of manuscript—its worktables—its floor space—in very much the same way as my father looked upon his shop in which he had his tombstones, his big trestles, his mallets and chisels, and his blocks of granite—my mother would smile, but would consider my proposition as another fantastic flight of the imagination. And yet, it seems to me, it is not fantastic. I am, or would like to be, a writer. And my own experience has been that a writer is, in every sense—particularly the physical one—a working man. And a writer, like other men who work, has a shop. And I am coming to you from the shop. And therefore, I am going to talk shop—because, it seems to me, it is likely to be the thing I can talk best, and that will be of greatest interest to you.

I wish I could tell you how to write stories in such a way that you could sell them for high prices to well-paying magazines. But the plain, bitter truth is that I can't tell you how, because I don't know how myself. I wish I could tell you how to write novels so that you could get them accepted by good publishers and enjoy a tremendous sale. But the plain and bitter truth again is that I can't tell you, because I don't know how myself. In fact, I don't think I even know for certain what a story or a novel is—a fact with which many of my critics would enthusiastically agree. I am constantly being fascinated and tempted by those glittering advertisements one sees so often in magazines today, showing a vigorous and keen-faced gentleman shooting his index finger out at you and saying: *"You* can be a writer too!"—and then going on to tell you how Chester T. Snodgrass of Bloomington took his course last year and found out about it in ten easy lessons in such a way that he *tripled* his income. Well, I'd not only like most earnestly to triple my income, but I should like most desperately to find out about it. And someday, I think, I am going to write that keen-faced gentleman with the index finger and enroll. But help of that sort, I regret to say, I cannot give you tonight, for help of that sort is not in me. A year ago, in fact, my agent called me up and in a trembling voice informed me that we had just sold a story to the *Saturday Evening Post*. The whole world reeled around us for a moment; then we became exultant. Our fortunes were made. It all looked so easy—we were on the line. The news leaked out, and friends would say to me: "I hear you've broken into the *Saturday Evening Post*," to which I would nod complacently, as if after all this was no more than was to be expected; and presently people were saying, "Well, I see you're a *Post* writer now—" at which I began to look and feel quite smug. My agent told me that the *Post* was so much interested in the story that one of its representatives had exacted from her a promise that she would not show the next story I wrote to anyone else before she had shown it to the *Post*; and we graciously consented to give them the first chance. Well, the upshot of it was, when I sat down and wrote another story, which we both gloatingly agreed was not only much better than the first story but had in it all the desirable elements that we thought a *Post* story should have—dialogue, characterization, and swift action; as for action we thought we had touched the peak, for I had the whole Battle of Chickamauga in. We debated whether we should let them have it for the same price as the first one, or whether the time had not now arrived—since I was an established *Post* writer — to demand Clarence Budington Kelland fees. We finally agreed that we would not be too severe, but would play them along diplomatically at first, and ask for only a thousand dollar raise or so. We thought it best not to hurry matters, and we agreed that it would probably be two or three weeks before we had their offer anyway. Well, we had their offer in six days — which was an offer of a flat rejection, with pained regrets that the story was not a *Post* story, and was lacking on the side of action. It was a stern blow, but we both recovered rapidly: the agent pointed out that there was still *Redbook, Collier's, Cosmopolitan,* and so on, in the high-paying class, and that on the whole it would be better to let *Cosmopolitan* or one of the other big magazines have it anyhow, so that it would get my name around more to the great public. Well, the story came bouncing back from one big magazine after another with the regularity of a tennis ball: we decided then to try "the quality group" — *Harper's, Scribner's,* and so forth — because by this time we had decided the story was a "quality" story anyway. No matter what it was, it kept bouncing back; and after my valiant agent had tried all of them — eight months later — we landed! We sold that story! We landed in the *Yale Review*! Now the *Yale Review* is an excellent publication — an admirable one — and anyone ought to be proud to be in it. But the difference, among other things, between being in the *Saturday Evening Post* and in the *Yale Review* is fourteen hundred dollars. I could have had a trip to Europe on the *Saturday Evening Post*, but all I got out of the *Yale Review* was an overcoat. I needed an overcoat very badly, and I spent all of my *Yale Review* check on the overcoat, and I got a good one. It was an English Burberry, solid wool and very thick, and it cost one hundred dollars. And then, just when I got the overcoat, we had no winter. It didn't go below freezing the rest of the time. Anyway, I've still got the over-coat.

But you see, if you expected to get someone out here who could tell you how to write a story, and how and where to sell it to a high-paying magazine, you've come to the wrong man. You should have got that keen-faced fellow with the index finger who can tell you how. The most I can promise you is that if you ask me how to write a story that will get into the *Saturday Evening Post*, I will tell you how, and then you will wind up in the *Yale Review*. Perhaps this has its value, too; for it has occurred to me that the next time I want to sell a story to the *Saturday Evening Post*, I shall start out by writing it for the *Yale Review*.

I am thirty-seven years old, and for the past ten years, at least, I have been writing for publication. For the last nine years all my income, in one way or another, has been derived from writing. I think I can truthfully say that I have not only lived for writing, but I have also written to live. It's all I had to live on: I had no other source of income—if I was going to keep on writing, I had to live by it. I had to support myself. And yet, I can also truthfully say that, so far as I know, I have never written a word, a sentence, or a paragraph, with the im-mediate objective of making money out of it. Please don't think I'm being snooty. I wish to God I did know how to go about deliberately coining words and sentences and paragraphs into immediate and productive cash. I'd love it. That's why I'm so fascinated by the keen-faced gentleman of the index finger—his talk of "publics," "slants," and "writing for your market," fascinates me. But, thus far, it is all Chinese to me. I don't know how to go about it.

I can also say this truthfully. In the last few years I have re-jected a number of offers that would have given me a great deal more money than I have ever had. I understand that my name as a writer is fairly well known, and one of my books, at least, two or three years ago, got pretty prominently into the bestseller list. But I counted up my total earnings, over the past ten years, since I began to write professionally, the other day, and found that they did not total forty thousand dollars. That's a lot of money—a lot more than most writers ever earn —and I certainly am not disappointed or depressed about it. But, on at least one occasion, I could have earned more than that total sum in one year's time if I had accepted employment that was offered me in Hollywood. I didn't take it. Why? I hasten to assure you that it was not because I was being noble. I have listened to writers who had a book published shudder with horror at the very mention of Hollywood—some of them have even asked me if I would even listen to an offer from Hollywood—if I could possibly submit my artistic conscience to the prostitution of allowing anything I'd written to be bought in Hollywood, made into a moving picture by Hollywood. My answer to this has always been an enthusiastic and fervent *yes*. If Hollywood wants to prostitute me by buying one of my books for the movies, I am not only willing but eager for the seducers to make their first dastardly appeal. In fact, my position in the matter is very much that of the Belgian virgin the night the Germans took the town: "When do the atrocities begin?"

But when I got an offer to go there and work, I did not take it, although it would have paid me more money than I had ever earned from writing in my whole life before; and I repeat again I have never felt noble about it. I did not go because I did not want to go. I wanted to write: I had work to do, I had writing, and still have, and I think will always have, that I wanted to get done. It meant more and it means more to me than anything else I could do. And I think that is the reason I am a writer.

Which brings us, it seems to me, to a somewhat deeper and more fundamental level—doesn't it? I have told you that I had to write to live—that if I go on writing, I must supply the sheer physical necessities of life out of the writing that I do. In one way or another, I have got to be paid for it; because I have no other money on which to live—and if writing as a means of support fails me, then I shall have to turn to other means that do not. And yet, even if that happened, I believe that, in some way, I would contrive to get my writing done. Because, from what I have told you, you will see that it has been in my life not only a physical and economic necessity; it has been, much more than that, a spiritual one. Why? That is what, with your tolerant permission, I'm going to try to tell you tonight; for it seems to me that if I can tell you anything at all that will be of any value or interest to you, it will in some way be tied up with this.

And it seems to me that if I can say to you what I want to say, it may be important, also, in a larger sense. I mean a sense larger than the mere facts of personal autobiography, which are relatively unimportant; a sense larger than the mere fact or chance or accident that I am a writer, or some of you will be lawyers, doctors, engineers, or business men. I think that if I can say the thing, it may be of some importance and some value to you because it will represent the experience not only of one man, but, in a certain measure, the experience of every man; because if I can tell you honestly and truthfully about my own work, about the changes and developments that have come about in it, I can also tell you something about the changes and developments that have come about in me—about my own connection with the world, about what I think and feel and believe about my work, and about the world, for if the work a man does is living work—work in which his mind, his spirit, and his life are centered—then it seems to me his work may also be a window through which one looks at the whole world. And writing *is* my work, it *is* my life—just as law and engineering may be yours—and because it is, everything I know and think and now believe is somehow vitally connected with this work I do.

Twenty years ago, when I was seventeen years old, and a student at Chapel Hill—which is the University in my native state of North Carolina—I was very fond, along with many of my fellows, of talking about my "philosophy of life." We were very earnest about it. It seems to me that we were always asking one another about our philosophy of life. I'm not sure now what mine was at the time, except that I am sure I had one. We were deep in philosophy at Chapel Hill—we juggled about such formidable terms as "concepts," "moments of negation," and so on, in a way that would have made Spinoza blush; and if I do say so, I was no slouch at it myself. It would surprise many people today to know that at the age of seventeen I had an a-1 rating as philosopher—"concepts" held no terrors for my young life; I could lead with a "concept" and counter with a "moment of negation" in a way that would even put Joe Louis to shame: I could split a hair with the best of them, and now that I have gone in definitely for boasting, I made a *one* in Logic, and it was said it was the only *one* that had been given in that course for twenty years. So you see, when it comes to speaking of philosophy, there is one before you who is privileged to speak.

I don't know how it goes with students of this day and

generation here in Indiana, but I know that to the students twenty years ago at Chapel Hill, "philosophy" was a most important thing. We stayed up nights and talked about it. We discussed the idea of God most earnestly: truth, goodness, beauty were our meat. We had ideas about these things, and, believe me, I do not laugh at them today: we were young, we were impassioned, and it was not bad. One of the more memorable events of my college career occurred one day at noon, when I was coming up a campus path and encountered coming toward me one of my colleagues whom I shall call B. C. Jones—largely because that happens to be his name. B. C. Jones was also a philosopher, and the moment that I saw him coming towards me I knew that B.C. Jones was in the throes. B. C. was red-haired, gaunt and angular, he had red eyebrows and red eyelids—he had come from a family of primitive Baptists before he came to Chapel Hill—and now as he came toward me, everything about him, hair, eyebrows, eyelids, eyes, freckles, and even the knuckles of his large and bony hands, were excessively and terrifically red.

He was coming up from Battle Park, which was a noble wood, in which we held initiations and in which we took our Sunday strolls. It was also the place where we went alone when we were struggling with the problems of philosophy. It was where we went when we were going through what was known as "the wilderness experience," and it was the place from which triumphantly, when "the wilderness experience" was done, we emerged. B. C. was emerging now: he had been there, he told me, for the past eighteen hours. His "wilderness experience" had been a good one—he came bounding toward me like a kangaroo, leaping into the air in intervals, and the first and only words he said were: "I've had a Concept!" And then he passed—he left me stunned and fastened to an ancient tree, as

B. C. went on down the path, high-bounding, kangaroolike, every step or two, to carry the great news to the host.

And yet, I do not laugh at it. We were young men in those days, but we were earnest and impassioned ones, and each of us had his philosophy. And all of us—this was the sum and root of it—had his "Philosopher." He was a noble and a venerable man—one of those great figures that almost every college had some twenty years ago, and that I hope they still have. For fifty years he had been a dominant and leading figure in the life of the whole state: in his teaching he was, I think, what is known as a Hegelian—I know the process of his scholastic reasoning was intricate—and came up out of ancient Greece through a great series of "developments" to Hegel—and *after* Hegel—he did not supply the answer, but *after* Hegel was our Old Man.

Looking back, all that does not seem important now—our philosopher's "philosophy." Looking back, it seems at best a tortuous and patched-up scheme. But what was most important was the man himself: he was a great teacher, and what he did for us, what he had done for people in that state for fifty years, was not to give them his "philosophy"—but to communicate to them his own alertness, his originality, his power to think.

To us, he was a vital force, because he supplied to many of us, for the first time in our lives, the inspiration of a questioning intelligence. He taught us not to be afraid to think, to question; to examine critically the most venerable of our native superstitions, our local prejudices, to look hide-bound conventions in the eye and challenge them. In these ways, he was a powerful and moving figure. Throughout the state, the bigot hated him; but his own students worshipped him to idolatry. And the seed he planted grew—the deposit of his teaching stayed—even when Hegel, concepts, moments of negation, had all gone, or had merged back into the confused and tortuous pattern from which they were derived.

About this time, I began to write. I was editor of the college paper—which, in my day, and under my direction, always did have, at least, a certain archaeological interest—since it was interesting to examine in this week's edition the ruins and relics of last month's news. But in addition to this, I wrote some stories and some poems for the magazine of which I was also a member of the editorial staff.

The War was going on then; I was too young to be in service, and I suppose my first attempts creatively may be traced to the direct and patriotic inspiration of the War. I remember one, in particular—a poem, I believe my first, which was aimed directly at the luckless head of Kaiser Bill. The poem was called defiantly "The Challenge," and I remember it was written in the style, and to according the meter, of "The Present Crisis," by James Russell Lowell.

I remember further that it took a high tone from the very beginning: the poet, it is said, is the prophet and the bard—the awakened tongue of all his folk—and I was all of that. In the name of embattled democracy, I let the Kaiser have the works, and I remember two lines in particular that seemed to me to have a very ringing tone—"Thou hast given us the challenge—pay, thou dog, the cost, and go!" I remember these lines so well because they were the occasion of an editorial argument at the time: the more conservative element on the editorial staff felt that the words "thou dog" were too strong —not that the Kaiser didn't deserve it, but that they jarred rudely upon the high moral elevation of the poem, and upon the literary quality of the Carolinian magazine. Above my own vigorous protest, they were deleted.

I also remember writing another poem that year, which was the spring of 1918, about a peasant in a Flanders field who ploughed up a skull, and then went on quietly about his work, while the great guns blasted far away. I also remember a short story—my first—which was called "A Cullenden of Virginia"—which was about the recreant son of an old family who recovers his courage, and vindicates his tarnished honor in the last charge over the top that takes his life. These, so far as I can recall them, were my first creative efforts; it will be seen what an important part the last war played in them.

I mention all this just to indicate what has happened to me in the last twenty years, and because of its reference also to a charge that has sometimes been made by some of my friends. One of them, for example, not more than three or four years my senior, is very fixed in his assertion of what he calls "the lost generation"—a generation of which he has been quite vociferously a member, and in which he has tried enthusiastically to include me. "You belong to it, too," he used to say. "You came along at the same time. You can't get away from it. You're a part of it whether you want to be or not"—to which my vulgar response would be: "Don't you you-hoo me!"

If my friend *wants* to belong to the Lost Generation—and it really is astonishing with what fond eagerness those people hug the ghost of desolation to their breast—that's *his* affair. But he can't have me. If I have been elected, it has been against my will; and I hereby resign. I don't feel that I belong to a lost generation, and I have never felt so. Furthermore, I doubt very much the existence of a lost generation, except insofar as every generation, groping, must be lost. In fact, it has occurred to me recently, that if such a thing as a lost generation does exist in our own country, it is probably more those men of advanced middle age who spoke the language, and who know no other now, than the language that was spoken before 1929. These men indubitably are lost. But I am not of them, and I don't think I was ever part of any lost generation anywhere. The fact remains, however, I was lost. And the fact that I no longer feel so is what I am going to describe.

It is a little premature to start summing up one's life experience at the age of thirty-seven, and I certainly do not intend to do so here. But, although thirty-seven is not a very great age to have learned many things, it is time enough to have learned a few. Rather, it seems to me, by that time a man has lived long enough to look back over his life and see certain events and periods in a proportion and a perspective he could not have had at the time when they occurred. I think that has happened to me, and since each of those periods really represent to me a pretty marked change and development not only in my whole view about the work I do, but in my views on men and living and my own relation to the world, I am going to tell about them now.

For the sake of convenience, I am going to begin at the time when I was about twenty years old, because I suppose that is about the age of many of you who are here tonight. Furthermore, it is a convenient date because it marks the date of my graduation from college, and the time when I was just beginning to hint timidly to myself that I might one day try to be professionally a writer. At that time, I did not dare go further than suggest this ambition to myself in the most hesitant and tentative fashion, and that period of hesitancy and reserve was to continue for at least six years before I ever dared to commit myself boldly and wholeheartedly to the proposition that I was a writer, and that henceforth *that* should be the work I did. Therefore, that first cycle, from about 1920 to 1926, it the one I am going to tell you about first.

Looking back, in an effort to see myself as I was in those days, I am afraid I was not a very friendly or agreeable young man. The plain truth of the matter is that I was carrying a chip on my shoulder, and I suppose I was daring the whole world to knock it off. The chip on my shoulder had, of course, to do with writing, and with the life I wanted to lead. And I suppose the reason I was outwardly so truculent at times, and inclined to be arrogant and take a very high tone with people who, it seemed to me, doubted my ability to do the thing I wanted to do, was that inwardly I was by no means so arrogantly sure that I could do it myself. It was a form of whistling to keep one's courage up.

When I was graduated from college in 1920 — I was then really just nineteen — I don't suppose it would have been possible to find a more confused or baffled person than I was. I had been sent to college in order to "prepare myself for life" — as the phrase went in those days — and it almost seemed that the total effect of my college training was to produce in me a state of utter unpreparedness. I had come from one of the most conservative parts of America, and from one of the more conservative elements of American life. So far as I know, all of my people until a generation before had been country people, whose living had been in one way or another derived out of the earth. Only within the past generation really had any of them "moved into town," and become business men — lumber dealers, contractors, and so forth. My father himself had been all his life a working man. He had done hard labor with his hands since the time he was twelve years old. He was a man of great natural ability and of a great deal of natural intelligence, and like many other men who have been deprived of the advantages of a formal education themselves, he was ambitious for his son, and wanted him to have one. It is but natural that people of this kind should endow formal education with a kind of magic practicality: a college was a kind of magic door which opened to a man not only all the reserves of learning, but provided him with a kind of passport to success, a kind of magic key to the great material rewards of place or money that the world has to offer. Further, it is but natural that a man like this should seek for that success along one of the roads that had always been approved, and the road that he chose for me was law. I think he had himself cherished all his life an ambition to study law, and I think he had always regretted the accident of birth and necessity that had prevented him from studying it, and in a way I had been chosen as a kind of fulfillment of his own ambition. By 1920, it was already apparent that whatever I would be, I would never be a lawyer. By that time my father was old and sick, and had only a year or two more to live, and I knew that I had grievously disappointed him. For that reason alone, it was difficult to admit, even to myself, the stirrings of a desire to write; and the first admission that I made to myself was an evasive one. I told myself that I wanted to go into journalism, and the first work that I looked for was newspaper work. Looking back, the reason for this decision now seems transparently clear: I doubt very much that I had at that time the burning enthusiasm for newspaper work that I thought I had, but I convinced myself that I did have it, because newspaper work provided me with the only means I knew whereby I could, in some fashion, write, and earn a living.

To have confessed openly to my family at that time an outspoken desire to be "a writer" would have been impossible. And the reason why it would have been impossible was that in their consciousness—as well as in my own— "a writer" was a very remote kind of person, a romantic figure like Lord Byron, or Longfellow or—or—Irvin S. Cobb—who in some magical way was gifted with the power to write poems and stories and novels that were printed in books or in the pages of magazines like the *Saturday Evening Post*—and who, for all these reasons, was a very strange, mysterious kind of person, who lived a very strange, mysterious and glittering sort of life, and who came from some strange and mysterious and glittering sort of world, very far away from any life or any world that *we* had ever known.

That, I believe, represents pretty accurately the image we all had in our minds about "a writer"—and I believe it represents pretty accurately the image many people have today. I don't think my own family, for example, have ever quite recovered from their own astonishment that I was, or was said to be, "a writer"; and if I had openly announced my intention of being one at the age of twenty, they would have been decidedly alarmed. And the reason they would have been alarmed —and later on were alarmed, when I did announce it—was that the whole thing would have seemed so fantastic and improbable to them. To be a writer was, in modern phrase, "nice work if you could get it"—if you could be a writer like Lord Byron or Longfellow or Irvin S. Cobb—but for one of the family, for a boy who had grown up in the town of Asheville, North Carolina, in Buncombe County—who had, it is true, *sold* the *Saturday Evening Post* on the streets of Asheville (if *that* was any sort of training for a writer)—now to openly assert he *was* one, or was going to be, bordered on the fringes of lunacy. It harkened back to the days of Uncle Greeley, who spent all his time learning to play the violin, and who borrowed fifty dollars from Uncle Jim one time to take a course in phrenology. I had always been told that there was a strong resemblance in appearance between myself and Uncle Greeley, and now I knew if I confessed my secret desires, the resemblance would seem to be a great deal more marked than ever. Well, it was a painful situation; it was, in many ways , an amusing one—it seems to me to be always such a human and American one, and it must be familiar to you all. At any rate, it was to shape the course of my life for years. That summer after graduation things turned out fortunately for me so that I got money whereby I could go to Harvard, and enroll in the graduate school for a year. And after that year was over, I managed to get money to go there for two years more, so that I was there for three years in all. Looking back upon that experience, I can see it now in a clearer perspective. At the time, I don't think I knew clearly my reason for wanting to go to Harvard, except that I was still marking time, and couldn't clearly decide what I did want to do. But I argued strongly for the Harvard move on the ground that it would give me the chance to do graduate work and to get a graduate degree, both of which, I argued, would be useful to me no matter what I later did. The real reason was that I wanted to write, and this move, groping as it was, was nevertheless some further effort toward it. At Chapel Hill I had begun to write one-act plays under the direction of Professor Frederick Koch, who had come there while I was a student and established the organization which has now become widely known as The Carolina Playmakers. Several of these plays had been produced there by the Playmakers with some success, and now, at Harvard, it was not only natural but almost inevitable that I should seek for admission in the late Professor George Pierce Baker's Forty-seven Workshop. Thus, it turned out almost immediately that my graduate work at Harvard developed mainly into the business of writing plays—although it is true I took some other courses and picked up a Master's degree more or less incidentally, on the way.

From this point begins a newer development. At Harvard, for the first time in my life, I was thrown into the company of a group of sophisticated young people—at least, they seemed very sophisticated to me in those days. Instead of people like myself, who had felt within themselves the timid but unspoken flutterings of a desire to write, and to be a writer, here were people who openly asserted that they were. They not only openly asserted that they were, but they openly asserted that a great many other people that I had thought were most dismally were not. I began to discover that when I made some hesitant effort to take a part in the brilliant conversation that flashed around me, I must be prepared for some very rude shocks. For example, it was decidedly disconcerting to a Chapel Hill youth of twenty years, when he eagerly asked another Harvard youth of not much more than that: "Have you ever read Galsworthy's 'Strife'?"—to have that other youth raise his eyebrows slowly, exhale a slow column of cigarette smoke, shake his head slowly, and then say in an accent of resigned regret: "I'm sorry. I can't read him. I simply can't read him. Sorry—" with a kind of rising inflection, as if to say it was too bad, but that the situation simply could not be helped.

They were "sorry" about and for a great many other things and people—too, too many, it now seems as I look back, for it seems that there was hardly a leading figure writing for the theatre in those days who escaped their censure. Shaw, for example, was "amusing"—but he was not a dramatist, he had never learned how to write a play; O'Neill's reputation was grossly exaggerated—his dialogue was clumsy, and his characters stock types; Barrie was insufferable on account of his sentimentality; as for Pinero, Jones, and others of that ilk, their productions were already so dated that they were laughable—in fact, almost everyone was out of step, one gathered, except our own particular small groups of Jims. And our own particular small group of Jims were by no means sure of one another —it was usually a case of "everyone's wrong but thee and me, and even thee is for the most part wrong."

In a way, this super-criticality was a very good thing for me. It taught me to be a good deal more critical and questioning about some of the most venerated names and reputations of the day, whose authority had been handed down to me by the preceptors of the past, and which I had accepted in too unquestioning a way. But the trouble with it was that I was now tied up in the speeches of niggling and over-refined aestheticism, which, it seems to me, was not only pallid and precious, but too detached from life to provide the substance and the inspiration of high creative work.

It is interesting to look back now and to see just what it was we did believe ten or fifteen years ago—these bright young men and women of the time, who wanted to produce something of value to the arts. We talked a great deal about "art and beauty"—a great deal about "the artist"; it now seems to me that on the whole the total deposit of this was bad. It was bad because it gave to young people who were deficient in the vital materials and experiences of life, and in the living contacts which the artist ought to have with life, the language and the formulas of an unwholesome preciosity.

We talked about "the artist" a great deal too much; looking back, it seems to me that the creature we conceived in our imagination as "the artist" was a kind of aesthetic Frankenstein. Certainly, he was not a living man. And if the artist is not first and foremost a living man—and by this I mean a man of life, a man who belongs to life, who is connected with it, and who draws the sources of his strength from it—then what kind of man is he?

The artist we talked about was not this kind of man at all; indeed, if he had any existence at all, except the existence that we gave him in our conversations and in our imaginations, he must have been one of the most extraordinary and inhuman freaks that nature ever created. Instead of loving life and believing in life, this artist we talked about hated life and fled from it; for that, indeed, was the basic theme of many of the plays we wrote—the theme of the sensitive and extraordinary person, the man of talent, the artist—crucified by life, misunderstood and scorned of men, pilloried and driven out by the narrow bigotry and mean provincialism of the town or village, betrayed and humiliated by the cheapness of his wife, finally, crushed, silenced, torn to pieces by the organized power of the mob.

This artist that we talked about so much, instead of being in union with life, was in disunion with it; instead of being near the world, was constantly in a state of flight from it. The world itself was like a beast of prey, and the artist like some stricken faun was trying to escape from it. The total result of this was inevitable: it was to develop a kind of philosophy, an aesthetic, of escapism. It tended to create in the person of the artist not only a special but a privileged character, who was not governed by the human laws that govern other men, who was not subject to the same desires, the same feelings, the same passions—who was, in short, a kind of beautiful disease in nature, like a pearl in an oyster.

The effect upon such a person as myself may also easily be deduced. Now, for the first time, I was provided with a kind of protective armor, a kind of glittering and sophisticated defense which would shield my own self-doubt, my inner misgivings, my lack of confidence in my own powers, my ability to accomplish what I wanted to do. The result was to make me arrogantly truculent where my own desires and purposes were concerned. I began to talk the jargon as the others did, to prate about "the artist," and to refer scornfully and contemptuously to "the bourgeoisie"—the Babbitts and the Philistines —by which, I am afraid, we meant almost anyone who did not belong to the very small and precious province we had fashioned for ourselves.

And, I am also afraid, that although we spoke about "art," "the artist," and the work we wished to do in phrases of devotion and humility, there was not so much of either one in us as there was of snobbishness. We felt superior to other people, and we thought we were a rare breed; because one cannot really be superior without humility and tolerance and human understanding, and because one cannot be of a rare, higher breed without the talent and the power and the selfless immolation that true power and talent have, I think most of us deceived ourselves. We were not the rare and gifted people that we though we were.

At any rate, so armed and so accoutered in the aesthetic garments that were fashionable at that time, I left Harvard and for several years I lived and worked in New York, supporting my body by teaching school in the daytime, and my soul by writing plays at night. During all this time I cannot say that things got better with me in my relation to my work and to the world. If anything, I think I became more truculent, for I was up against it now—I no longer had the soothing assurance of support from home, or the comforting agreements of sophisticated colleagues in the Harvard Yard. I was living all alone in the big city, earning my living, and trying to make

my own way; and for the first time in my life, as far as my
work and my ambitions were concerned, I was right up
against it. In blunt phrase, I had to "put up or shut up" — not
only to justify myself in the eyes of the world, but to justify
myself in my own belief and faith and conviction and self-
respect. That is certainly a hard time in the life of any young
man — particularly of any young man who is trying to create.
It certainly ought not to be ridiculed or laughed at, and I do
not do so now; for the man is right up against the naked facts
of self and work — there is nothing beyond himself that can
help him, his strength is in himself, and he has to pull it from
himself; and if he cannot, there is no other hope for him. But
it does explain also a good deal of the truculence and the arrogance of youth: its furious distemper, its conflict with the
world. With me, the period was a time of stress and torment,
for I had now committed myself utterly — there was no going
back, no compromise, and my position was a desperate one.
The result was I had pulled up my roots bodily, broken almost
utterly away from my old life — from my family, my native
town, my earlier associations — there was nothing for me now
except myself and work. I suppose the almost religious belief I
have in work may date from just this period; for I think it was
the fact that I could work that saved me. The fact also was, I
wanted to work, and felt that I had work to do; and I think
that was also a fact of great importance — for, as I was to find,
and as I already suspected, there are so many people who want
to write, but who do not want to work; there are so many
people who like to talk about being an artist without ever
going to the tremendous expense of spirit, energy, and concentration that one has to go to if he is an artist. So that
period, although still a confused and tormented one, and in
some respects a mistaken one, was not by any means a wasted

one; for in that time, I began to learn the great necessity of work.

My personal happiness did not grow any better; if anything it grew worse, because for several years after I left college I knew nothing but failure and rejection. I was still trying to write plays—although it was largely chance and accident that had led me to writing plays, I was now fanatically convinced that plays were all that I could ever write, were all I cared to write, were what I had been destined by nature to write—and that unless I could write them, and succeed with them, my whole life was lost. This was not only wrong—it was as fantastically wrong as anything could be: whatever other talents I had for playwriting—and I think I had some—the specific requirements of the theatre for condensation, limited characterization, and selected focus were really not especially for me. Even my plays at that time showed unmistakably the evidence of my real desire—for they abounded in scenes and characters, a great variety of places and of people, too great a variety, in fact, for the economic and commercial enterprise of the theatre profitably to produce. Something in me, very strong and powerful, was groping toward a more full, expansive, and abundant expression of the great theatre of life than the stage itself could physically compass: it was something that had to come out sooner or later, as a pent flood bursts above a dam—and in 1926 I found it—and another cycle had been passed, another period of development begun.

I was in Paris in the summer of that year and, the beginnings of my plan now working in me, I bought a tablet and began to jot notations down. I simply jotted down on the pages of this tablet—without plot or plan, and often without order—a sequence of the things that I wanted to put into a book. In the autumn of that year I went to London, and stayed there several months, and it was during this time that I began the actual composition of the first book I ever wrote. When I returned to America early in the following year, the beginning of the book was written. I continued with it in New York day by day, working meanwhile at the University where I had been formerly employed. The first draft of the book was finally completed in 1928, and after vicissitudes and disappointments which I shall not attempt to tell of here, but which led me to believe at last that I had failed, and had even deluded myself for all these years with the notion that I was a writer, the manuscript was read by a publisher, who wrote me about it immediately—I was in Vienna at the time. When I returned to America, I went to see the publisher, and after some discussion the book was accepted. For the next few months I worked upon rewriting and revision, and in the fall of 1929, the book was published, and another stage in my experience had been passed; and still another begun.

It has seemed to me for some time that there is a kind of significance in the fact that my first book appeared in October, 1929. For me, it seemed that in a way my life—my working life—had just begun; but in so many different ways I did not know about, or even suspect at that time, so many things that I believed in, or thought that I believed in, were ended. Many people see in the last great war a kind of great dividing line in their own lives—a kind of great tale of two worlds, a world before the War, and a world after the War; but in my own experience, if I had to write my own tale of two worlds, I think I should be more inclined to use 1929 as the dividing line. Certainly, that has been the most memorable division in my own life that I can now recall.

Before that, as we have seen, my experience as a man and as a writer had passed through certain well-defined stages, all of which were very familiar to the times and to the lives of many other young men of the times. The son of an average small-town family, I had in the early twenties embarked upon a writing career—had decided to be a writer—a fact which was not only in complete variance with the lives of all my other people before me, but was also symptomatic of a marked social tendency of the time—the desire of thousands of young men everywhere to write. I had passed through progressive stages of change and of development which were also characteristic of the time: I had gone through the stage of aesthetic preciosity, of talking about "art" and "beauty," and about "the artist"; of scorning "the bourgeoisie," the Philistines and Babbitts, who were not only not artists, but who could never understand "the artist," but belonged to a completely different, separate world. From this, which was a time, I am afraid, in which I talked a great deal more about "beauty" and "art" than I created it, expended a great deal more time in scorning and in ridiculing "the bourgeoisie" than in trying to find out who they were and what they were like—I passed into the period when I had to go to work, and where I learned for the first time what work—hard, creative work—was like, and where at last I began to spend more time in an effort to create "art" and "beauty" than in talking about it. And now finally, I had reached the stage of first accomplishment—where at last I had accomplished something, got it completed, accepted, printed, and put between the covers of a book, where for the first time the general public, if it so desired, could look at it.

This is certainly a definite and closely linked chain of clear development, and for me it marked the end of one great cycle. Although perhaps I did not know much in 1929, I did know a good deal more than I knew in 1920. I knew, first of all, that writing was hard work—desperately hard work—and whoever accomplishes a good piece of writing must work hard and constantly, with exhausting concentration, and not depend upon sporadic flashes of casual inspiration to do the job for him. I knew furthermore, and finally, that I could write—that I was able to see a job through to the end, and able to get it published by a good publisher. It is not necessary to point out what an inestimable comfort this knowledge was to me, for it had served to establish some confidence in my own abilities which I had never had before, and to restore my self-respect and my belief in myself and in what I wanted to do, which had been shaken by years of failure and frustration. I was certainly a wiser man in 1929 than I was in 1920, and I think I was also a stronger and surer one. I no longer had so big a chip upon my shoulder, I was no longer so truculent and occasionally arrogant in my relations to other people, because I no longer felt such inner need to prove to myself that I could do what I wanted to do. But I suppose a good deal of the old foolishness still remained: I would have smiled in 1929 at some of the aesthetic snobberies and preciosities of the young men at Harvard in 1923, but if anyone had asked me why I wrote, why I wanted to be a writer and continue to write books, I would have said some of the same things that I had said years before: I would have talked about "the artist," and I suppose I might still have had a romantic and fanciful notion of him, and of his relations to society. I am afraid I might also have talked a good deal about "art" and "beauty"—perhaps I shouldn't have been so hard on "the Babbitts and the Philistines," and as arrogantly scornful of "the bourgeoisie" as I had been in 1923—but I would have still looked down on them from a kind of aesthetic altitude and felt that they belonged to a separate order of things, in a different world. I was a lot closer to life, to people, to the world around me, to America in 1929, than I had ever been before; although I was still too detached from it, not nearly close enough. But the experience of the last few years — the experience of work — the necessity of work — the fact that I really had worked had now brought me much closer to life, much closer to an understanding of the lives of people, as I think work always does. And for the last three years, before the publication of my first book, the work I had been doing had taught me much — that work, in substance, had demanded a kind of spiritual and emotional excavation of the deepest and intensest sort into the life I had known and of which I had been a part — the life of my home town, of my family, of the people I had come from — of the whole structure and frame of things that had produced me. I knew more about all of this than I had ever known before, but, as I was to discover, I did not know enough. For one thing, the book still showed unmistakably the evidence of the stages I had gone through, the periods of development, the special aesthetic faiths and creeds of the time. It is what is called an autobiographical novel — a definition with which I have never agreed, simply because it seems to me every novel, every piece of creative writing that anyone can do, is autobiographical. Nevertheless, it is true that this book was autobiographical in the personal and special sense: it was possible, for example, to identify the life of the hero with the life of the author — to suspect that a great many of the characters and incidents in the book were drawn pretty closely and directly from the writer's own experience. And, although I have not read the book for years, I believe that in this sense of the word — in this special autobiographical sense — was the book's greatest weakness: I believe the character of the hero was the weakest and least convincing one in the whole book, because he had been derived not only from experience but colored a good deal by the romantic aestheticism of the period. He was, in short, "the artist" in pretty much the Harvard Forty-seven Workshop sense of the word—the wounded sensitive, the extraordinary creature in conflict with his environment, with the Babbitt, the Philistine, the small town, the family. I know that I was not satisfied with this character even at the time: he seemed to me to be uneasy and self-conscious, probably because I was myself uneasy and self-conscious about him. In this sense, therefore, the book followed a familiar pattern—a pattern made familiar by Joyce in *A Portrait of the Artist as a Young Man*, and later in *Ulysses*—a book which at that time strongly influenced my own work. But I think the book also had been conceived and created with some of the blazing intensity of youth: although I did not know it at the time, in that sense of the word the book was a kind of passionate expletive—a fiery ejaculation hurled down upon a page of print because it had to come out, it had to be said. Here, too, my real education was beginning, for as yet I did not know these things. Again, the book had a rather extraordinary career: although it was on the whole well-reviewed and well-received throughout the rest of the country, and had, for a first book, a moderately good sale, in my own home town it was received with an outburst of fury and indignation that in my own experience has not been surpassed, and that I believe is even extraordinary in anyone's experience. Briefly, the people of the town read the book as if it had been the pages of the *World Almanac*; and seeing that some things were true, they became almost immediately convinced that everything was literally true and literally intended; and from this they became so outraged that they denounced me and my book individually and in the mass—from the pulpits, from the street corners, and from the public press; in letters signed, and in letters anonymous; and in threats that included tar and feathers, hanging, gun-shot, and all other forms of sudden death. Their outrage and anger, although mistaken, were unmistakable: there is no doubt that from the moment of the book's publication, I became an exile from my native town. I could not have come back at that time, and it was seven years, in fact, before I wanted to come back, and did return.

This was bewildering and overwhelming: it was all different from what I had expected — so different from the reception that I had hoped to have in my home town that for a time my own sense of grief, disappointment and chagrin were very great; for one of the things it is hard to lose is the desire for the approbation and applause of one's own neighbors — the knowledge that one has succeeded in the estimation of the people of his own town. Moreover, it did do something to strengthen me in a further belief in what was perhaps the fundamental theme of the whole book — the story of the sensitive young man in conflict with his environment, driven out at last, forced to flee and escape from his own town. For now that had happened to me, and if that had been all that had happened, it might have embittered me into further belief and confirmation of my earlier error. Fortunately, there were other compensations: if I had been driven out at home, I had been accepted elsewhere; if my own townspeople had read my book with outrage and indignation, the larger public had read it as I had intended it to be read, as a book, as a work of fiction, as a product of the creative imagination which, if it had any value at all, had value because it was just as true of Portland, or Des Moines, of people everywhere, as it was of my own town.

So there I was in 1929, at the end of one route, at the beginning of another, at the end and the beginning of so many different things I then did not know or suspect, that looking back now, I seem to have been a guileless innocent. On the whole, my view of things was pretty hopeful, pretty cheerful, for although I did have the desolating and rather desperate sense of exile, of having pulled up my roots completely as far as the old life was concerned, I had a feeling now of new beginning, too—of being launched at last, of having before me the happy prospect of an established and productive career. At that time, among the many other things I did not know, I did not know that for a man who wants to continue with the creative life, to keep on growing and developing, this cheerful idea of happy establishment, of continuing now as one has started, is nothing but a delusion and a snare. I did not know that if a man really has in him the desire and the capacity to create, the power of further growth and further development, there can be no such thing as an easy road. I did not know that so far from having found out about writing, I had really found out almost nothing: I had made a bare beginning, I had learned at best that I could do it. I had made a first and simple utterance; but I did not know that each succeeding one would not only be harder and more difficult that the last, but would be completely different—that with each new effort would come new desperation, the new, and old, sense of having to begin from the beginning all over again, of being face to face again with the old naked facts of self and work, of realizing again that there is no help anywhere save the help and strength that one can find within himself.

Again—and now I was moving to another deeper stage—I had not realized yet that the world changes, that the world is changing all the time, that the world, indeed, is in a constant and perpetual state of revolution—and that a man, a creative man most of all, if he is going to live and grow, must change with the world. I did not realize, in fact, even in 1929, that those images and figures of my experience and training—the

image of "the artist" and of "art," of "beauty" and of "love,"
of the wounded sensitive, driven out and fleeing away from
the Philistines of the tribe—all of which had seemed so fixed
and everlasting in the scheme of things, were really just the
transient images of the times, a portion of the aesthetic belief
and doctrine of the period. I did not realize that the year 1929,
which was so important to me in such immediate personal
ways concerning my own life and my immediate career, was
to be a fatal and important year in so many other ways I did
not even know about at that time, in so many ways affecting
the life of the nation and of all the people in it, affecting human beliefs, that it seems now to mark a dividing line between
two worlds. About the organized structure of society in 1929
—its systems of finance economy, politics and government—
and how they shaped and affected the lives of people, I knew
almost nothing, and had never considered it a part of my interest to question or examine them. Certainly, if anyone should
have suggested to me, in 1929, that it was not only a part of
the purpose and function of an artist to examine them, but
that if he continued to produce, his participation and examination would be inescapable, I should have denied the proposition utterly. I should have said that the purpose and the function of the artist was to create, to create what was true and
beautiful, without reference to its social implications as regards the world around him; I think that I should probably
have further said that the interest of the artist in such things as
economics, politics, government, the organized structure of
society, was not only outside the province of his life and work
—to create the beautiful and true—but would probably be
alien and injurious to it, if he allowed it to intrude in what he
did.

The fact that I no longer feel this way, and how and why,

and by what degrees and stages I have come to feel differently, marks the last stage of my development at which I have now arrived, and I am going to try to tell you about it now.

When I went abroad, for a year's stay, early in May, 1930, some seven months after the publication of my first book, the great American depression was already well under way. And yet, my life was still so absorbed with matters of more personal and immediate interest to me that I had very little idea of what had happened. True, I was aware that there had been a "crash" in Wall Street—a whole series of them—for I had been in New York when they had occurred, and, in one way or another, a great many of the people that I knew were involved in them. In a general way, I was aware that almost everyone was involved, because I had become conscious in the past few years, while I was absorbed in my own work of creation, that there had been a general widespread change in lives of people everywhere, of no matter what walk or station. In later years, certain unforgettable memories would come back: I could remember a day in Vienna in October 1928, when the market was at its peak: a group of Americans, men and women of middle age sprawled out on the seats of a big sightseeing bus, outside of a tourist agency, everyone of them absorbed in the stock page of the Paris edition of the New York *Herald Tribune*. And I remember going home to North Carolina, in the summer of 1927, I believe, and discovering with a sense of shock that a great many of my friends—young men of about my own age—were more feverishly in contact with one element of New York life than I was: there was a stock ticker in a broker's office in one of the office buildings in the town— something I had never known there before—and it seemed to have become a kind of rendezvous of many of the younger people, who were combining their speculation in the local real estate market—for the town itself was in the throes of a fever-ish boom—with speculation in the New York market. And everywhere around me there were flashes, picked up here and there, day after day, that indicated to me that something was happening to the whole country and to all its people that I had never known before: one would see taxi drivers buried in the latest stock reports; newsboys were familiar with the latest prices; at the city university where I taught, some of the in-structors were speculating with their slender salaries. I caught the fever very strongly from some of my own friends. Two of them, young men whom I had known at Harvard, were now employed writing programs for the radio, and they were quite seriously involved in the market, as were most of their friends; and I remember one very well, a young man who had been an actor, and who was now a director in the radio, but whose main interest now had become his speculations in the market, which were said to have succeeded fabulously, and already to have mounted to a great fortune. I remember how, when the "crash" came, he was wiped out overnight; and then, he just bled very quietly to death—it only took a few days, but he started bleeding from his veins, and they could not stop it; the blood soaked out like water through a sponge until the man was dead; and I remember his funeral—or rather his funeral services—for everyone was very modern in those days, and wanted to avoid the protracted horror of a burial; so all his friends were called up and told that everything was going to be very casual and pleasant—that "Tony would like it better that way"—and that "the services would be very short"; and they were—so short, in fact, they were over almost before one got seated; the preacher arose and spoke cheerfully for about five minutes, and said how happy Tony must be to know that all his friends were here, because his was such a bright and cheerful nature, etc.—and then it was all over, and everyone shook hands and filed out and no one even mentioned the fact that Tony was dead—and there was nothing unpleasant there to remind us that he was, because his body had been quietly cremated that morning. And I remember another man, a Wall Street broker, whose family I knew; they were the most fashionable people of my acquaintance, and now that my book was out, I was invited to dinner at the great apartment on Park Avenue; and there were brilliant and distinguished-looking men there, and the women were very beautiful and glittered, but the broker suddenly was all shriveled up: he had always been such a spruce and jolly-looking man, plump and ruddy with waxed moustache points like Otto Kahn's; now all this was gone except the moustache points. He had just collapsed like a balloon; even the plumpness and the ruddiness had gone out of his cheeks, until now they were withered like an old apple, and he sat there huddled by the fire in the living room of his great apartment, with all the brilliant and glittering people moving about him, an old man with a rug about his shoulders, with the maids bringing him things in glasses which he took: and you could just see something oozing out of him as he sat and shook and dwindled there before the fire.

Yes, I had seen all these things by the time I went abroad in 1930, but as yet it was their personal tragedy or drama, not their wider significance, of which I was aware. And looking back, I cannot say that any of my intellectual or artistic contemporaries were any more aware of what had happened than I was. There was still a large expatriated colony of Americans in Paris: some of them had come back recently, and the burning intellectual issue of the day was classicism versus romanticism. In fact, on the night I sailed for Europe, which was May 9, 1930, this issue was reaching its climactic apogee; for a group of our most brilliant moderns were meeting Professor Irving Babbitt in debate at Carnegie Hall—the future of culture was at stake, and that night the great issues that might determine the whole course that the arts must take were to be stated and defined.

As for myself, I was thinking of another book, and of the fact that I had let some months elapse since the first one had appeared, and had been so immersed in the turmoil of my own emotions—the huge disturbance my first book had created at home—that I had done very little toward the second one; and I was conscious now of the fatal impingement of time: a sense of pressure, and the knowledge that I must get to work at once, make good use of my year abroad—I was going by the grace of Guggenheim—and have a new book finished, if I could, by the time I came back. I suppose if I thought anything about the existing crisis in the nation's finance, I thought of it as a specialized and localized thing—something which largely affected a place called Wall Street and a special group of people who did business there. But I did not understand in what manifold and complex ways those strands were meshed into the whole web; I had been in New York and had seen the spectacular and dramatic flashes of explosion, but the dull thundering detonations that were later to come, the sight of the whole mass slowly detaching itself and rumbling down in dusty ruin was yet to come. I did not know of it; I did not foresee it—Mr. Hoover was still around giving reassurances from time to time, and confident the worst was over. May, June, July—the early summer passed in Paris; and I worked. I saw a few Americans, two young women and their brothers who were on a jaunt; one of the men had grown a beard, and it had turned out fiery red, to everybody's huge amusement; they lived in a little, very cheap but very good, hotel on a square behind the Bibliothèque Nationale; the weather was lovely, and there were trees and a little fountain in the square; and I would go there almost every day for lunch; and one of the girls had learned to make deliciously cold and heady cocktails in an enormous silver shaker from a formula she had invented herself; and after this, we would all go down and have lunch on the sidewalk in front of the little restaurant downstairs; and amuse ourselves watching old, old men tottering back and forth with great loads of books across the endless tiers of the great Bibliothèque; and, what was most amusing, watch other men, both young and old, go in and out the doors of the sumptuous and celebrated brothel just to one side of the Bibliothèque which is known as the House of Nations; and after we had eaten, the man with the red beard would get out his accordion, which he had learned to play in a few week's time; and he would play it, and sometimes we would sing; and later on I would go back home to work, and the others would separate and go to various places; we would make arrangements to meet again that evening. It was a very pleasant summer.

Later on, in July and August and September, I was in Switzerland; and I had a room in a small but very clean hotel at Montreaux, and my room had a large stone balcony, and down below there was a lawn that was a sheet of velvet, and flowers seemed to have been embroidered there, and all this stretched directly to the lake, which was fifty yards or so away, and of a blue incredible; and across the lake, on the French side, were the Alps that you had to look at twice before you believed they were there; and even then you didn't quite believe it; and it was very quiet, a few casual and intimate voices of people down below, and of the kitchen help; and every now and then the great, fast thrash of the paddles as the lake steamers, white and clean as swans, came into the landing down below, disgorged and took on, and then, with startling speed, were on their way again. Meanwhile, I worked upon my book, and occasionally I saw Scott Fitzgerald, who was living at Vévey, a mile or two away, and two or three times, when Swiss cooking got too dull, I would take an airplane and fly to France, where the cooking was not dull, to Dijon, or to Lyons, even to Marseilles. So the summer passed. Late in September, early autumn of that year, I was in the Black Forest, in Freiburg. It is a lovely city, and the country all around is a haunted and enchanted one; I remember being in a country inn towards sunset, and watching the slant of light on mown fields, cool, darkening up the slopes of the Black Forest; and I remember how some cows ran through an arch and out upon a road, a straw-haired boy of fourteen whacking them upon their stringy dung-spattered behinds; I remember the dry, hard, wooden sound their hooves made as they came into the road, and there was everywhere around a clean pervasive smell of hay, of stables and manure. I remember the people were excited, for the time was approaching for the great Wahl — or national election — and I remember the excitement of election day in Freiburg; and there were over twenty parties running; and keen interest in the Nazis and the Communists; I remember that that year the Communists got four million votes.

Early in October, I was in England, saw my publisher, and other people that I knew, and now for the first time, I heard the sound of the dull, the muffled detonations. For the first time heard that there were breadlines in America, and that there had been riots, that already conditions in some places were desperate; and I remember hearing my publisher, a young man who, I think, had never liked America very much, say grimly: "It's going to be bloody! Bloody! They are cruel people over there—they'll let their people die! It's going to be bloody, wait and see!"

Other people were excited and surprised. What was happening in America? they would ask me. For years they had heard of America's fabulous prosperity, of high wages, of carpenters and factory-hands who rode to work in motor cars. And now, with explosive suddenness, they were reading that these same people were starving, were standing in long queues along the streets to get a mug of coffee and a crust of bread. How could this happen? they asked me, and I, too, was dazed. Everything had happened so explosively, and I had no answer, except suddenly it came to me that things do happen with explosive suddenness in America: the way spring comes, for instance, exploding from the earth overnight, the way it goes just as suddenly, and summer is there. And now, it was not spring or summer: these were over, there was desolation, cold and bitter want at home.

One morning in November, I awoke to look out on dumb yellow fog, and to find that the ruin had come at last to my home town. That morning there was a small item in the *Daily Mail* announcing that the bank at home had failed; and knowing this meant ruin to many people that I knew, I cabled. Soon I had a letter, giving fuller details of the bank's failure and the town's collapse—a failure and collapse that had been surpassed in magnitude in the nation's history, because the town is not a large one, but never in completeness or extent. The bank had gone down, carrying with it the government, the business, the commercial and industrial life of the whole town. As the details poured in, there was revealed a picture of catastrophe—a picture of the whole corrupted web, the huge honeycomb of speculation, paper, inflation and deceit—which, with enthusiasm, and a measure of restraint, had mounted, mounted for ten years through all the successive stages of public drunkenness and hysteria. And now the whole thing was in ruins — not only the life of the town, but the lives of all its people: it was an appalling microcosmos of the whole breakdown — in feverish miniature, a picture of the whole boom that had swept the nation. And now, like the man I had known a year before in New York City, hundreds of people I had known all my life bled quietly to death. The whole town bled to death: dozens of people took their lives in those first weeks, dozens died from shock, from grief, from defeat, from disappointment and despair; and thousands more with all life taken from them were left to live. I sent money to those I could help, the winter passed, I worked upon my book, and early in the spring, in March the following year, I went home.

The scene had changed: it was as if a bleak gray weather had come into the lives of everyone. Everywhere around one now one heard of nothing but the tragedies of the so-called depression. The change in intellectual life was also vast — in many respects, it seemed to me, it was too sudden. Young men of brilliant minds and talents who had been vigorously debating the merits of classicism and romanticism ten months before, who had for years lived a life of disdainful expatriation, had overnight, it seemed, become learned economists. Their language and ideas were now not only wholly new, but it was impossible to gather that they had ever had any different ones. They spoke of the revolutionary movement as if they had been suckled at its breast, since they were babes in arms; they were themselves derisive of the little schools and cliques of obscure cults and writings of which they had themselves been just ten months before the most productive part. One such, whom I had met a few months previous in Paris, and who had come home with me on the boat, was indicative of the suddenness of these conversions: his own career had illustrated aptly the dilettantism of the time before. The descendant of an enormously wealthy family, he had passed successively through the stages of Greenwich Village, the Left Bank, and little magazineism. He had run a bookshop for a while and had endowed with his own funds one of the better-known obscure little magazines of the time. He had been the hero—or the villain—of a celebrated novel of the twenties, which had dealt with the lives and adventures of young drunken people in Paris and in Spain. And at the time I met him, even at the very moment of our arrival back in New York, he was neck-deep in the Palestine movement: he had just returned from there, he was writing articles about it, his whole life and faith and energy was now given to this cause. Within three weeks of my return I heard from him again. He invited me to a party at his place in Greenwich Village; and now again, the man's horizon had all changed. When I came in, he asked me what I had been doing and I told him I had been writing. "Writing?" he said inquiringly, puffed meditatively on his pipe a moment, and then smiling tolerantly, he said: "You writers." "What do you mean 'you writers'?" I demanded. His use of the pronoun was surprising, for only three weeks before he had certainly, by his own proclamation, been one himself. "I mean," he explained —"how can anyone possibly be interested in writing books when there are so many other things to do? Besides, how can you writers write about anything when you know nothing about economics?"

Yes, the effrontery of it was appalling, but it had happened. Within three weeks' time, the ex-Left Banker, little magazine-er, café-drinker, and Palestine movementer had become a world economist. He had fallen in apparently with an extraordinary character who called himself an engineer, and who said that the only hope of the world was for the engineers to take charge of it and plan it out anew along the lines of technical economy. By these means, with the potential wealth existing in our resources, in our inventions and discoveries, and in our means of production, it was possible for every man to live like a king in his own right — to have the equivalent of fifteen thousand dollars a year. Our new convert, however, had not only lapped all this up, he had improved upon it; and within four weeks he had his own book ready, which blandly set up a new world of economy, based on technical means, which promised everyone the equivalent of twenty thousand dollars a year. So, he was off on a new track; but really, it seemed to me, very much the same track he had always been on.

The effrontery, and what seemed to me also to be the bland dishonesty, of these quick conversions disgusted and repelled me. But, it was nevertheless manifest that something in the structure of the life around us was seriously amiss. I had seen the evidences of collapse in the collapse of my own town; and now new evidences were coming to me day by day. For the first time in my life I began to examine critically the life around me — to ask for the reason behind the fact. For the first time, the assurances of well-fed people began to look and sound spurious in the face of suffering and starvation that one saw everywhere. It was no longer enough, for example, to be told that "these depressions have always been, and are bound to recur from time to time" — that explained nothing; besides that, it was in direct contradiction to the boast that some of the most knowing of these epople — a professor in the Harvard Business School had been one of them — had made to me only a year and a half before: that there would never again be another depression, that the cycle of "prosperity" had been permanently insured, that modern business and finance methods had now learned to control these things in such a way that they could never happen. And now they were not only happening, but they were happening to a degree that they had never happened before; and the vaunted system which had been able to prevent them was now not only unable to prevent them, but lay itself in ruins, with its chief directors calling for help. It was no longer enough to be told, when one saw shabby and battered men begging for a cup of coffee or for ten cents, the reason these people begged was because they wouldn't work; it was no longer enough to be told that these people would not take work even if it were offered them, because this was no longer true, if it had ever been. More than this, even with those shipwrecked men that one saw along the Bowery, along the waterfront, in City Hall Park, huddled in doorways or squatting in the foul congestion of public latrines, sometimes stumbling blindly with the poison of cheap drink, sometimes incoherent of tongue and addle-witted, it was no longer enough to be told that these men were nothing but stumble-bums, that they would only take the money that one gave them to buy more drink with, that we had always had such people, that we always would. It was no longer enough to be told these things, because for the first time in my life I wanted to know, in the name of God, why? I was working furiously on a new book — really, a work of tremendous exploration and excavation — discovering, for the first time, the look of things, the feel of things, the size, shape, smell and taste of things, particularly here in America: it had all suddenly exploded into my consciousness with a kind of intensity and significance it had never had before — I was crystallizing for myself the whole material picture of the universe, of the world around me — the great job now was just to dig it up and get it down, get it down—somehow record it, transform it into the objective record of manuscript—even upon thousands and thousands of pages that would never be printed, that no reader would ever see, that would never be framed into the sequence of a narrative—but at any rate, now would be *there* at last upon the record—worth all the labor of the effort just so long as I could get it down, get it down.

And that enormous task of excavation, of exploration and discovering, went on for four years in Brooklyn, while slowly the structural lineaments of a book appeared. Meanwhile, through work, through the marvelous vitalizing power of work, through the intensity of my own effort, the world kept soaking in. It kept soaking in like light out of the dull gray weather, like sunlight in the month of May, like small, fine moisture, like a steady rain. Young men were writing manifestos in the higher magazines of Manhattan, but the weather of man's life, the substance and the structure of the world in which he lives, was soaking in on me in those years in Brooklyn, in those countless days and hours spent in my room, above my table, looking out the window, walking the endless jungle of the streets, talking to men all night in all-night coffee-shops, in subways, along the waterfront, upon the bridges, in South Brooklyn, upon trains, in the cinders of day coaches going west, in rooming houses in Washington, from my own people, and the story of their own ruin, which was the town's, from everything I'd ever seen or felt or known or heard about, now coming in upon me the way things must, not learned by a lightning stroke from Heaven, by a swift conversion from the Mount—but soaking in like cold gray weather, soaking in like cold gray rain, soaking in with my own life and breath and and work and blood and pulse, and the desperation of my own endeavor—to get it down, just get it down: a deeper furrow of the plow, a deeper bite of the drill, another depth, another level I had never touched before. And it was this:

My job was done in 1935—the job on which I had been busy for four years—and suddenly I knew that I was through with many things. I knew that I should never write, or want to write again, the kind of books that I had written before. I had wanted to follow the book I had completed with a book about a love affair, about a woman, and about a young man in the city: for two years I had poured my energy and talent into the composition of such a book, and now I had what I had, I knew what I knew—and I was done with it. It was really not farewell to love—but it was farewell to the way I had felt about it. Just as the individual conflict, the pain and suffering of a sensitive young man at odds with life, and with the forces of family in his native village, no longer seemed so important to me as they had before, so did the individual ecstasies or heartbreaks of a love affair between a man and a woman not seem as memorable and as universal as they once had. It was not that I now despised these things, or thought that they were contemptible: I recognized their validity, and the important place they have always had and will continue to have in the lives of men, but my circle had widened, the range of my interest had increased immeasurably—those four years of work, of discovery, of exploration and of recording, of letting the weather of life and of humanity soak in upon my conciousness, had taken me out of the more narrow provinces of myself and of my work, of personal happiness or frustration, the vanity and the preoccupation of my view.

From this time on things mounted quickly to a head.

All of my life ever since childhood, I had wanted what all men want in youth: to be famous and to be loved. Now, I had

had them both and — there is not time or need here for apology or equivocation — I can only say that, so far as I was concerned, they were not enough. And I think, if we speak truth, the same has been true of every man who ever lived and grew, and had the spark of life and growth in him. It has never been dangerous to admit that fame was not enough — it has, indeed, by one of the greatest poets who ever lived been called the "last infirmity of noble minds" — but it has been, for reasons that I cannot say, or at any rate, shall not mention here, been dangerous to admit the infirmity of love. And yet — or so it seems to me, as a simple product of what I have myself known — there may not have been a grown and a living man who has never known the knowledge that love brought him; but there cannot be a grown and a living man who has not escaped the circle of its small, tight whole.

Perhaps, the image of it may suffice some people; perhaps, as in a drop of shining water, love may hold in microcosmos the reflection of the sun and the stars and the heavens and the whole universe of man; and mighty poets dead and gone have declared that this was true, and people have professed it since. As for myself, I did not find it so, nor, plainly, do I think a frog-pond, or a Walden Pond, contains the image of the ocean, even though there be water in both of them.

Both images, indeed, went back through all the steps, the degrees, the shadings of my education; and what we had been taught we should believe. "Love is enough, though the whole world be waning" — it may have been, and yet I doubt it: as for myself, I did not find it so.

And fame? She was another woman (of all love's rivals as I was to find, by a strange paradox, the only one by woman and by love beloved) — and all her shifting images, and all the guises of her loveliness, phantasmal, ghost-wise, like something flitting in a wood, I had dreamed of since my early youth—until her image and the image of the loved one had a thousand times been merged together. Now, I had her, as she may be had—and it was not enough.

These relics of the past were there. But life's weather had soaked in, and yet, I was not conscious yet what seepings had begun, or where, in what directions, the channel of my life was flowing. I was exhausted from my labor, respiring from the race, conscious only as is an exhausted runner that the race was over, the tape breasted, that he had won. This was the only thought within me at the time: the knowledge that I had met the ordeal a second time, and finally had conquered—conquered my desperation and my own self-doubt, the fear that I could never come again to a whole and final accomplishment.

The circle goes full swing. The cycle draws to its full close. For four months, emptied, hollow, worn out, my life marked time, while my exhausted spirit drew its breath. And then the world came in again, upon the flood tide of reviving energy. The world came in, the world kept coming in, and there was something in the world, and in my heart, I had not known of before.

I had gone back for rest, for recreation, for oblivion to that land which, of all the foreign lands that I had known, I loved best. I had gone back to it in hours of desperate confinement, of brain-fagged searching, in retrospect, in imagination, and in longing a thousand times from the giant jungle web of Brooklyn. I had gone back to it a thousand times, as men in prison pent, haltered to all the dusty shackles of the hour, the confused traffics of clamorous days, the wearying grayness of inevitable now, have longed for Cockaigne, for the haunted woods, the enchanted meadows, and the faery flood, the cloven rock. I had gone back to it in ten thousand dreams and memories of time and of desire—the sunken bell, the Gothic town, the plash of waters in the midnight fountain, the Old Place, the broken chime, and the blond flesh of secret, lavish women. I had gone back so in my memory and in desire a thouand times to Germany: and now that spring I was really there again—and no man ever had a happier or more fortuitous return.

Byron, they say, awoke one morning at the age of twenty-four, and found himself a famous man. Well, I had to wait some ten years longer, but the day came when I walked at morning through the Brandenburger Gate, and into the enchanted avenues of the faery green Tiergarten, and found that fame—or so it seemed to me—had come to me. For two months or more I had been away from home, had seen no papers and read no letters, had sought to find some easement, some slow and merciful release of the great coiled spring that was my mind and heart and very life that had been stretched to breaking point for years. And I found it now in a series of oblivious wanderings that had led from Paris to Kent and from the Romney marshes up to London, and from London to the flat fecundity of Norfolk, and from Norfolk to the small and tidy smugness of the Dutch, and from Holland, as the train bore on, across the great and fertile tillage of Westphalia, to Hannover, old time-haunted town, and there across the kiefern-haunted forest of the North to vast Berlin. And now May had come again, and I walked below the mighty blossoms of the great horse chestnut trees, and through the Brandenburger Gate, and through the arcades of enchanted green, and felt, like Tamerlane, that it was passing great to be a king, and ride in triumph through Persepolis—and be a famous man.

After those long and weary years of Brooklyn and brute labor—of desperation and the need for proof to give some easement to my tormented soul—it was the easement I had dreamed of, the impossible faery, so impossibly desired, and now brought magically to life. It was—it seemed to be—the triumph and the glorious vindication of all that I had thought my life could be, that man could work for, or art achieve. The news of my success at home had come to Germany— where already I had been known for three years, and had achieved celebrity—and now, it seemed to me who had so often gone a stranger and unknown to the great cities of the world that now the whole of it was mine. The great town, the whole world was my oyster. Letters were there for me, and invitations: it seemed they had been waiting for me—and for three weeks there was a round of pleasure, celebration, the wonderful thrill of meeting in a foreign land and in a foreign tongue a hundred friends, now for the first time known and captured—and May, and the cool nights, the glorious freshness of the air, the awakening of spring, the enchanted brevity of northern darkness, and glorious wine in slender bottles, and morning, and green fields, and pretty women—all of it was mine now, it seemed to have been created for me, to have waited for me, to exist and live in all its loveliness for my possession.

Three weeks passed so. By day there was the shining and the sapphire air, the horse chestnut trees, the singing sparkle of exultant life that swept through me across the town, so that at noon among the great crowds thronging the Kurfürsten-damm, I also was a part of the green faery of the great Tie-garten park, and thence unto all crystal sparkles of Berlin, until I seemed to share it all, and all of it to be in me, as but a single, shining and exultant drop of water reflects and shares, and is a part of the million, million scallop shells of dancing light, and every lapping wave, and every white sail on the surface of the Wawnsee.

And there would be the singing of the air by day, the unheard singing of the blood, and the great crowds thronging
the Kurfürstendamm, the gay and crowded terraces of the
great cafes, and something, half-heard, half-suspected, coming
from afar, a few flung seeds of golden music upon the air, the
sudden music of the tootling fifes, and suddenly, the solid, liq-
uid smack of booted feet, and young brown faces shaded
under steel goose-stepping by beneath the green arcades of the
Kurfürstendamm, the army lorries rolling past, each crowded
with its regimented rows of young, formal, helmeted, arm-
folded and ramrodded bodies, and laughter, laughter in the
crowd, and laughter rippling like a wave across the terraces of
great cafes, and bubbling like wine sparkles from the lips of all
the pretty women — and all the singing and the gold of it was
mine.

But something happened — I was not prepared. Too much
gray weather had soaked through into my soul, and I could
not forget. The memory of unrecorded days, the renaissance
of brutal weathers, the excavation of the jungle trails — it all
came back to me again insensibly, soaked through the shining
brightness of that air, came through the latches of those clack-
ing tongues, forced through at last its grim imponderable into
the contours of those shining surfaces, the sense of buried
meanings which not even May and magic and the Kurfürsten-
damm could help.

Sometimes it came to me with the desperate pleading of an
eye, and the naked terror of a sudden look, the swift conceal-
ment of a sudden fear. Sometimes it just came and went as
light comes, just soaked in, just soaked in — words, speech and
action, and finally in the mid-watches of the night, behind
thick walls and bolted doors and shuttered windows, the con-
fession of unutterable despair, the corruption of man's living

faith, the inferno of his buried anguish — the spiritual disease and death and strangulation of a noble and a mighty people.

And then day would come again, the cool glow of morning red, the bronze gold magic of the kiefern trees, the still green pools of lucid water, the faery stillness of the park and gardens of the great Tiergarten street — but none of it was the same as it had been before. For I had become aware of something else in life, as new as morning, and as old as Hell, and now articulated for the first time in a word, regimed now in a scheme of phrases and a system of abominable works. And day by day the thing soaked in, soaked in until everywhere, in every life I met, and in every life I touched, I met and saw and knew the ruin of its unutterable pollutions; and it still came in, it kept coming in, so known now and understood at last beyond all depths of intellectual understanding, since the cancer and the root both came out of the body I had loved.

And now, another layer had been peeled off the gauzes of the seeing eye; and something had come into life that I had never seen before, but that now once seen and understood, I could never forget or be blind to again.

When I went back to America — to New York — the Fourth of July, my new-won fame was waiting at the boat, and, more faithful than with most, she abode with me through the winter of the furious season — but something cold and clear had come into my vision, and she no longer looked the same. Here, too, with this new mistress, I learned to see anew the world, and, seeing what fame was — such fame as I had won — and how desolately different from the goddess I had fancied her to be, I was not blinded. I saw that I had thought since childhood that she was the goal of my intent, and I saw I was mistaken. And with that further loss, I gained, as with all losses now, new hope: from every desperation came a fresh beginning, from every province of my exile, a new land. And I think I should be very grateful to her, for through her now the world that we have made, the structure of this life as we have fashioned it to be, came to me in a series of merciless revelations: and all the falseness of its false pretense, the easy barter of its given love—so lightly won by the moment's notoriety, so quickly vanished by the moment's loss—together with the huge conspiracy of the parasite—the whore, the harpy, the thief, the lawyer, the ambitious and the fashionable fool, the blackmailer, the contriving parasite—all rushing in like body lice, to suck and batten on the blood that fame has fattened. The ordeal began—two years and more of it—and through it all in law, in court, in finance, in business, and society I came to know the corrupt and shoddy counterfeits of man. And, curiously, I was not disheartened. Curiously, I was not embittered, because for the first time in my life I was seeing clear and whole; and through the very failure of the thing I had so wanted to achieve, I was finding out at last the structure of things as they are. From this grim loss, and from the desolation of these new discoveries, I had derived, by a strange paradox, a new sense of life, a newer and, it seems to me, a better hope. For at the bottom of the well, at the rock bottom of the soil, in the whole corrupt and shoddy structure of the upper honeycomb, I had begun to see and understand and feel the common heart of man, and finally, I had come to see that this, no matter how much it gets betrayed, is the thing that can never be betrayed; no matter how much it gets corrupted, is the thing that finally can never be corrupted; no matter how much it gets defeated, is the thing that can never be defeated— the thing that is rock bottom at the end—the thing that will remain, that changes and is yet unchangeable—that endures and must endure.

· W R I T I N G   A N D   L I V I N G ·

The people! Yes, the people! The people that cannot ever be defeated or betrayed—the betrayed and the defeated people, the corrupted and the misguided people, the duped and superstitious people, the inert and the submissive people—but in the end, always the people!—just the people!—the rock bottom of the invincible and the everlasting people!

The rich people, yes!—The society people, yes!—The fashionable people, yes!—The fame-hunting and celebrity-chasing people, yes!—The pretty, reputation-loving, and bed-sleeping women, yes!—The publishers with their folk-lore and their mythology of benevolent and art-loving paternalism, yes!—The politicians and the rabble-rousers and the far-seeing statesmen, yes!—The people gathered together at cocktail parties, talking about the latest plays, the latest books, the latest ideas, the latest talk, all in the most approved fashion, yes!—The college professors and instructors all talking their own varieties of the latest and most approved talk, yes!—All that they have come to be, all that the moment's fashion, or that the moment's need has made of them, all that they said, or thought that they thought, or felt that they felt, or believe that they believe—the whole systems of patterns that the structure of life which they have created and in which they have existed, have made all of them!—I had seen and known them all now, in the cycle of my thirty-seven years—the dupe, the jester and the cheat; the snob, the parasite, the adept and the whore—all phases in the swing of the great cycle, all parts of it and the fame of things, and victims of it, and not to be hated or despised!—But at the end and always now, the eternal tide that changes always and that always is the same.

The people—yes, the people!—in the end, nothing but the people—on street corners and on the street, in subways and in crowded trains, in little towns and in great cities, at churches and at carnivals, upon the Eastern coast, and all across the continent — moving by day beneath immense and timeless skies, thronging the streets, the buildings, and the factories, the houses and the farms by day and all the million patterns of their daily schedules — but in the end, the only thing there is, the thing that lasts forever, and that cannot be betrayed — the people!

I had been long from home, and then one day I was home again. Eight years had passed, through the whole cycle of escape and flight, of exile and of desperate longing, of work, of failure, of accomplishment — I had lived my exile out in three thousand days and nights of exile and of desperate longing — of wanting to return until the very thought of it became an ache, the very fact of it a dream, a dream so intolerably vivid and intense that almost I could not believe it had ever been more solid substance than a dream. Oh, I had rebuilt it in my brain a million times — rebuilt it street by street, and house by house, and leaf by leaf, and stone by stone, until the very memory of all the faces burned there in my vision like the immortal memory of ghostly visitants from an unforgotten never-to-be-captured world — until I would awake and say — "There once was I — there once was such a boy as I — there once were certain people — such and such a town — there once this living flesh touched certain substances — there once this shoulder leaned against a certain tree — this foot was raised upon a certain step — there once this hand was grasped upon a certain rail — was clenched around a certain handle until almost I can feel the size and contour of its shape within my palm again — it must have been, it must have been — and yet — ?"

I would rebuild it so there in my brain a million times with all the vividness of exile and of intolerable longing, to return and think — "It must have been — it must have been — and yet, perhaps I dreamed it. So many sundering floods have passed between—so many cities, countries, foreign lands, strange tongues and faces—so many, many jungle depths of time in Brooklyn, of work, of desperation, of love, of death, renewal, and fatigue—so many million, million things have come and gone, begun and ended, whole tides of this swarming and imperial world have passed between, the surge of oceans, and the thrust of crowds, the forgotten memory of so many million, million men and words and facts and hours and places—it must be, yet it cannot—I have dreamed it: I'll go home again!"

Thinking—"I have a thing to tell them now—I'll go back again! I shall explain my reasons, and lay bare my purposes—reveal my life unto its heart's core, so nakedly that no man can doubt me! I'll go back some day and they shall hear me—we shall know each other utterly—they must understand! And I'll go back."

And seven years had passed, and I was long from home, and one day I went home again.

Ah well, well—dear friend, for here at this final hour, I turn to you in parting and farewell—you can't go home again: the tale is told now, the circle had full swing.

Hearing again the accents of remembered yesterdays, seeing again the fragments of the ruined town. "We're glad to see you—so you've come back again. We've missed you, now you ought to stay. Have you seen Bob yet? Jim's been looking for you. A lot of people ask about you. I know your family's glad to have you back. Sure; there was a lot of talk at first—a lot of them were pretty mad about the book—I guess you heard about it—but Hell! that's all over now! It's all forgotten; the only ones that are mad today are those who think you should have put *them* in. Here's Ed now: we're glad to see you. We've got the greatest place on earth — so come on back to stay!"

The ruined town! The new and splendid buildings, emptied even of the personnel they were to house — and shining tunnels, glittering with tile, that leap through mountains twixt the town and country where boys used to swim — the monuments of brief grandeur, "fragments to shore these ruins" — the blazing slope of concrete where the green hill was — and new stamped-out hotels, and arcades, shops and filling stations — the shining fragments of the ruined town! At night, the Parson smiles through his artificial teeth and strokes his lantern jaws reflectively as he looks out upon his ruined town. The hills are lovely, even in the darkness, in the month of May — there has never been a better year than this for dogwood, so the old men say. The Parson smiles and strokes his lantern jaws reflectively, as he looks out on his ruined town. Even the hills are lovely in the night — for on the hills, in mounting linkages, is sown light — and the splendid buildings, the million-dollar courthouse, the two-million-dollar city hall, bathed silently in secret, lighted night, just like the nation's Capitol at Washington, are modern, new, and, although unpaid for, imposing to a stranger. All impresses by its smartness now — even Parson's new police force, who are young men now, spruce, lean, well-kept young men, so different from their paunchy elders, so courteous to strangers when they park in the wrong place — such upstanding, spruce, clean-cut young men: Americans, of course, of the well-known Anglo-Saxon stock, and twenty-five years old, and with natty, neat, new uniforms of brown — brown well-pressed trousers and brown shoes, brown jaunty caps, brown neckties, crisp brown shirts, brown cartridge belts around the waist, and a whole arsenal of brown cartridges, a brown holster, and the brown butt-end of a most business-like six-shooter, hanging most formidably halfway down the brown thigh, and strapped around the brown leg with a brown thong — and with it all, such nice young men, so courteous, so attentive and well-spoken to strangers when they make mistakes — with something in their eyes, however. Here is one I used to know; we went to school when we were ten years old together, and we often shared our lunch, and he was pitcher, I was first base on the baseball team — and behind the smiles of greeting, something strange now, something changed through rigid pleatings of the mouth, the visage of the old lost boy looks forth again — and there is something in his eyes, something dead and hard and cold and furtive, in the eyes of of all these men in brown, that boys in school twenty years ago did not have. The cops have shining motors now — and often, in the quiet streets, in the still hours of the night, one will find them, two together, silent, hard-eyed, hurrying, waiting. The saxophones are moaning low out at the Country Club: the crowd is drunk, you can get good Scotch now, although some of them still stick to corn. Two country kids from Zebulon are sitting on the edges of their cells there in the splendid million-dollar county jail: they are coming round now, spitting through their bloody lips the fragments of their broken teeth and wondering just what happened, for young cops in brown can be emphatic when it comes to corn and kids from Zebulon; and in another cell, another disturber of the peace and menace to the public welfare is also spitting through his shredded teeth, more casually, less reflectively — for he knows by now what it is all about, and what he may expect from clean, upstanding brown-shirted cops who come upon a union organizer. Six hundred men, beneath the sweet young sod of May, are rotting in their graves tonight, and sixty-eight have shattered bullet fractures

in their skulls; all still below, and nothing stirs, except the turn-
ings of the mute, compulsive worm; and up above, along the
cool, leafed streets, all silent, too, ten thousand other men are
lying in their beds, and not as dead men lie, but with gaunt
sockets open, and the eyes a-stare in darkness, ten thousand
ruined men above the earth are lying in their graves as well.
Upon the dead controls of the dead town rests the dead, cor-
rupting tyranny of the Parson's dead, compulsive hand—
and the Parson smiles through artificial teeth upon his crisp and
young brown-shirted force of clean young men tonight, and
rubs reflectively his lantern jaws.

And I? "There was a boy—ye know him well, you hills —"
I had been long from home, and now I had come back again—
and what is there to say?

Time passes and puts halters to debate. There was so much
to say that could be spoken, there was so much to say that
never could be said—there was so much to utter, that all unuttered, in my longing I had heard it, all unspoken, spoken in
mute passages of three thousand days and nights of exile and
impossible desire—and now, I had come home again, and
what is there to say?

Feeling the foot again upon the stair, the creak of the old
tread, the sagging give of the old rail, feeling mute shapes in
darkness pass about me, the rustling of a leaf, the huge imponderable stillness of the night, the cool of huge-starred mountain night again, and also the awakened and unliving presences
of yesterday—thinking—"I have come home again, here is the
darkness, here the rail, here is the footstep, the tread—'there
was a boy—ye knew him well, you hills'—I was here, this
was I—"

Seeking to find him in the remembered street, looking for
him by the ancient tree, trying to find him in the old house—

the wind stirs, and darkness moves about us, and there is the still huge imponderable of night—"I was a boy here—where are the others—I was a boy here, this is I—"

You can't go home again.

To you, dear friend and parent of my spirit in my years of search, I say farewell. The circle ends full swing: this period of every man—a phrase in the great lexicon of what all living in the cycle now is ended, and I say farewell. I was the boy who put his foot upon the stair, I was the child who had his shoulder to the wheel. I was the youth of obscure parents who went out to learn of this land that is America. I knew the pride of youth, the suffering, the vanity, the egotism of youth, who knew its aspirations, its high endeavor; I was the youth who went the road and traveled the long route through arrogance and scorn, the preciosities of lifeless and life-hating aesthetics; I was the youth who spoke the phrases, who learned the language, and who tried to shore up the feeling of his own wounded loneliness, insufficiency and self-doubt with the protective words of arrogance and scorn; I was the young man who learned to work, and in his work found first accomplishment; I was the lover, the love-stricken, love's tragedian in the little universe of love, love's martyr, love's forlorn; I was the exile, and the desperate explorer, the son you fathered in his time of need, the one you shielded from his own self-doubt, the one you aided nobly and with generous unselfishness to the accomplishment of his own fulfillment; I was the man, for three years past, who founded on his own rock now, and now reliant on his own strength, knows now that henceforth he must find it only in himself because, like every man, he knows what he knows, he is what he is, he has what he has. And I know now that you can't go home again.

Therefore, dear friend, the time has come when each must

go his way—you to that life you know the best, and to which now the years, the peril of the time, the loyalties of your own affiliation, and your conscience have now fixed and destined you forever—and to the past, and standing there upon its known and familiar shores; and I to mine—upon another shore, and facing after all these lives and deaths and births of things, a new land, and another hope.